1969

3 0301 00041969 3

This book may be kept

~~~ ~EN DAYS

The American Crisis in Vietnam

THE AMERICAN CRISIS IN VIETNAM

by Senator Vance Hartke

The Bobbs-Merrill Company, Inc.
Indianapolis and New York

LIBRARY
College of St. Francis
JOLIET, ILL.

The author acknowledges with appreciation the permission to quote from the following works:

Alan Burnett Cole (editor), *Conflict in Indo-China and International Repercussions,* © 1956 by the Fletcher School of Law and Diplomacy, Cornell University Press; Martha Gellhorn, *A New Kind of War,* © 1967, The Manchester Guardian; Douglas Pike, *Viet Cong: The Organization and Techniques of the National Liberation Front of South Vietnam,* © 1966, The M.I.T. Press.

The Bobbs-Merrill Company, Inc.
A Subsidiary of Howard W. Sams & Co., Inc., Publishers
Indianapolis · Kansas City · New York

Copyright © 1968 by Vance Hartke
All rights reserved
Library of Congress Catalogue Card Number: 67-18650
Designed by Martin Stephen Moskof
Printed in the United States of America

959.704
H329

1-6-69 Strand Book $2.98

48789

to Martha

Acknowledgments

I would like to express my great gratitude to my legislative assistant Dr. Clair M. Cook, whose help on this book has been invaluable; to Robert Beeler, also of my staff; to Robert M. Ockene of Bobbs-Merrill; and to the very helpful staff of the Library of Congress, Miss Marjorie Browne in particular.

Contents

The American Crisis in Vietnam

Introduction

The people of Vietnam are suffering in a crisis whose magnitude is not, I believe, measurable by any index.

For the Vietnamese, after a quarter of a century of almost constant warfare, the current war of "attrition" is becoming a war of annihilation. For the Americans who have sustained losses, as those of us who have fought in America's other wars know, there is no adequate expression for the depth of the grief felt.

Since the United States is a major participant in the crisis in Vietnam, this is an American crisis. The United States has a responsibility to use her resources to bring the increasing devastation to a reasonable conclusion. The permanent end to the fighting must be based on the political realities of Vietnam.

All Americans are aware that this will not be a simple task because our adversaries are intransigent. However, we must not react to this intransigence of the other side with an intransigence and a lack of moderation of our own.

Each concerned American citizen is exercising his responsibility for the course of events in Southeast Asia. Over the past months, many of us have examined the depths of our consciences in order to decide what are the appropriate means to implement the goals and values which Americans share.

As an elected representative of the people and a member of the government, I have an added responsibility. I have the responsibility to stand up and to speak out for what I believe is right. I must give my analysis of the facts so that our democracy can function properly. I must unhesitatingly mark out the path which I believe should be followed to secure and advance the basic values which make us Americans.

The future for America will not be an easy one. Neither is this an easy path for an individual to follow. But I can do no less.

There are four considerations that make it particularly urgent to present these views at this time.

First, a majority of the American people have indicated that they do not understand exactly what we are fighting for in Vietnam. A public opinion survey of June 1967 revealed that only 48 per cent of the American people thought they knew what were the aims of the administration's policy in Vietnam.[1] But as the Harris poll published November 13, 1967 showed, 65 per cent of the American people wanted a change in that policy and only 23 per cent of them approved President Johnson's handling of the war.[2]

Any changes in American policy, such as a massive increase in the number of troops in Vietnam, will obviously be justified in terms of the American aims. Given these uncertainties about American policy, it is crucial that the public be given as much information as possible. Only then can the people participate actively in the decisions to be made on American aims and the use of American power.

Second, I was last chosen to serve in the Senate in the election of 1964. The programs and the Presidential candidates of the two parties in that election offered a well-defined choice to the American people over which direction our society should take during the next four years. The results of this referendum were as clear-cut as the choices presented. The vote in 1964 was an overwhelming endorsement for the domestic and foreign policies of the Democratic Party.

At home, we promised to increase the efforts undertaken during the Kennedy-Johnson administration to improve the lives of our citizens in this rapidly changing nation. We pledged to make these efforts our number one priority.

In foreign policy, we did not agree with those who were frustrated with a complicated world and yearned for a quick "victory." In a world in which our adversaries also possess nuclear weapons, there could be only one final and total solution to the problems which we face. That solution would be the nuclear incineration of civilization. We felt that a more moderate course could maintain the national interests of the United States.

On Vietnam, President Johnson said,

> Others are eager to enlarge the conflict. They call upon us to supply American boys to do the job that Asian boys should do. They ask us to take reckless action which would risk the lives of millions, engulf much of Asia, and threaten the peace of the entire world. Such action would offer no solution to the real problem of Vietnam.[3]

This was my position when I was a candidate in 1964. This was the position which the American people sustained at the polls. This has remained my position.

Whether I am branded a "nervous Nelly" or as someone who is advocating "childish divisive things," I shall continue to uphold, at whatever cost to myself, the commitments which the American public entrusted to her elected representatives.

Given the differences between the two Presidential candidates, it is disturbing that Senator Goldwater applauds the policies now being undertaken in Vietnam.[4] I may be assailed as a critic of the current policy. But this criticism should not overshadow the fact that I have consistently supported both the foreign and domestic programs on which I was elected and which I believe are right for America.

Third, as the casualty lists are growing longer, with no end to the fighting in sight, the impatience of the American people is mounting. Certain segments of the population are voicing the demand for a quick, easy military victory. The Republican governor of our most populous state recently expressed this emotion when he said,

> We don't have a foreign policy in California, but as a citizen, it just doesn't make sense to me for a great power to meet the enemy down on his level of jungle warfare . . . or to send million-dollar airplanes against bamboo bridges. We have the power to wind it up fast, and I think we should use it. I think Ho Chi Minh should be sitting on an apple crate, begging for help.[5]

I believe that such emotions are not a substitute for policy. Following that course would advance us farther down the road which, according to Secretary General of the United Nations U Thant, is already the initial phase of World War III.

Those of us who feel that such a course can only lead to disaster have an obligation to make our counsel heard in the public arena. For with the increasing American losses, the others will certainly not desist from presenting their criticisms and alternatives.

I think that the most basic desire of Americans is to achieve an honorable solution to the conflict in Vietnam which upholds the national interests of the United States. At the same time, many citizens are impatient that we are not reaching this goal. Some of those who are impatient advocate a quick military victory. But it is essential that we do not confuse this sentiment with the more general desire for an honorable settlement. The warm response shown by the public to the hope of American-Russian cooperation engendered from the Glassboro summit conference sustains this belief. I also feel that this public reaction surprised those who had been arguing that the basic American feeling was for a hard military policy.

Finally, the United States has undertaken certain vital commitments to the international "rule of law," in the often repeated phrase of Secretary of State Dean Rusk. These commitments must serve as the guidelines for the conduct of our foreign policy. They are the *only* basis for the hope of advancing the rule by law instead of the rule by force. These commitments are the highest expression of the ideals of the American experience.

These commitments do not comprise unilateral American responsibility to preserve world order. Rather, these commitments are contained in the American affirmation of the Charter of the United Nations. It should be noted that the principles of the U.N. Charter are reaffirmed in the preamble, in Article 1, and in Article 4 of the SEATO Treaty.

When the United States undertook the unilateral use of force in Vietnam, we violated our signed treaties—SEATO and the United Nations Charter. While our actions violated these commitments to international rule by law, our spokesmen continued to pay homage to the principle and to settlement of disputes by peaceful means. We should ponder the meaning of these commitments to which we so often refer and which we expect other nations to follow. These are some of the passages which appear in the Charter, to which we gave our signature on June 26, 1945:

"(Preamble) We the peoples of the United Nations determined to save succeeding generations from the scourge of war . . . to establish conditions under which justice and respect for the obligations arising from treaties and other sources of international law can be maintained . . . to practice tolerance and live together in peace . . . to ensure . . . that armed force *shall* not be used, save in the common interest. . . .

"(Article 1) The Purposes of the United Nations are: 1. To maintain international peace and security. . . . (Article 2) All Members *shall* settle their disputes by peaceful means. . . . All Members *shall* refrain in their international relations from the threat or use of force. . . . (Article 33) The parties to any dispute, the continuance of which is likely to endanger the maintenance of international peace and security, *shall,* first of all, seek a solution by negotiation, enquiry, mediation, conciliation, arbitration, judicial settlement, resort to regional agencies or arrangements, or other peaceful means of their own choice. . . . (Article 37) Should the parties to a dispute of the nature referred to in Article 33 fail to settle it by the means indicated in that article, they *shall* refer it to the Security Council. . . ." [Italics added.][6]

The current unilateral policy being pursued in Vietnam is clearly a flagrant violation of these legally ratified and binding commitments. If we ever expect other nations to follow these principles for the settlement of international disputes, then we must follow them now. If the United States is to contribute to the establishment of peace and world order, we cannot sanction a policy which, to borrow an historical analogy, turns these treaties into mere "scraps of paper."

Unfortunately, the crisis in Vietnam has produced attacks on the patriotism and loyalty of *certain,* not all, individuals who disagree with the current policy. There has even been an attempt to abrogate the rights of some such individuals to participate in the democratic processes of policy formulation.

Americans who understand the workings of a democracy are aware of the ultimate significance of these ideas. For example, on April 14, 1967 former Republican Vice President Richard Nixon called for an end to the criticisms of Vietnam policy made by certain Democrats. Mr. Nixon said that they were guilty of prolonging the war.[7] However, just three days later he indicated that he would continue to press for a sharp increase in American military efforts.[8]

Let us suppose for a moment that the proposal for increased military action is not the proper course to be followed. Let us take the hypothesis that the implementation of this policy would prolong the war and cause more American casualties. In that case, active support for such a policy would clearly not be in the national interest.

But who has the right to decide whether this policy or the policy of someone else is really in the national interest? According to the thinking expressed in his statements, Mr. Nixon is qualified as the censor of others, but there is no censor for him.

In other words, some people are allowed to disagree, others are not. But which people? Obviously, to this way of thinking, "I" am allowed to speak, "you" must keep quiet.

This is not the democratic way. It is at odds with every American tradition, the rights guaranteed in the Constitution, and the duty of every citizen who is concerned for his country.

The vast majority of Americans hold the same basic values. Our country is not divided ideologically. The members of the administration, my colleagues in the Senate who favor increased reliance on military power, and those of us who have urged more emphasis on the political realities of Vietnam are all working to secure and advance American interests.

It is a fact that certain people who have urged a de-escalation policy have been the objects of vigorous attacks. It is also a fact that those who have urged a more intense military policy—and therefore are also disagreeing with the current policy—have not had their loyalty impugned. No one has suggested that they be deprived of their rights and obligations.

Under no circumstances would I ever stand by while an attempt was made to abridge the rights of any American. To do so would be the epitome of hypocrisy. To do so would destroy the values for which we are now asking American boys to die. To do so, as shown by American history, is both impractical and impossible.

A variety of abuses have been heaped upon those of us who have consistently worked for a diplomatic solution in Vietnam.

We have been accused of not supporting the American soldiers in the field and letting "others fight" to protect us. We are accused of being "strangely silent" on the terrorist tactics of the Viet Cong, of allowing "the deeds of the Viet Cong [to] go largely unnoted in the public debate," of speaking only of the "escalation of our side," and of maintaining a "moral double bookkeeping." We are accused of wanting the United States "to tuck tail and run in Vietnam."[9]

These are some of the emotional charges that have been raised. What is the record?

I have stood fully behind every man serving in Vietnam. I now stand and will continue to stand fully behind these men. I would never do anything that would ask these boys to fight with "one hand tied behind their back."

I have voted for every military appropriation for Vietnam. I will continue to vote for these appropriations without exception. I will do my part to see that these men have every resource and supply that they need.

The question that is confronting us is not whether we should support the American soldiers in the field. There is a consensus among Americans on supporting these men.

It is a vast oversimplification to say that the only alternatives for a Vietnam policy are either to remain or to withdraw. The object of the debate going on among Americans is to determine which one of a number of policies we shall pursue in Vietnam. Advisers to the South Vietnamese? The enclave strategy? 500,000 American troops? 1,000,000 American troops?[10] Blockade Haiphong? Bomb the population of Hanoi?

I have never suggested that the United States should make a disorderly withdrawal, should "tuck tail and run." Because the particular policy pursued has changed over time, and because the various alternatives are always under review by the administration, all segments of the public have a right to participate in the judgment on which policy best serves the American national interest.

Many practices and values of the Viet Cong and of North Vietnam are repugnant to us. I am certainly not in sympathy with their philosophy and practice of government. I feel that it is highly regrettable that the genuine nationalist and anticolonialist movement of the Vietnam people has been led by Communists.

There is a consensus among Americans on the ideals and values which we support. There is a consensus among Americans on rejecting and opposing the practices of the Viet Cong and North Vietnam. However, there is no consensus on the proper means to carry out this opposition.

Our opposition to the Viet Cong and North Vietnam is only the basis for a policy: opposition *per se* is not a policy. The real issue which Americans are attempting to decide in the current debate is what is the best and most effective way to cope with the Viet Cong, North Vietnam, and—more importantly—the power of China.

In other words, we are in agreement on the ends which we seek. But there are serious disagreements on the appropriate policies, on the means, to achieve these ends. This is the real problem which the American crisis in Vietnam has raised in the public arena.

But precisely how are the people and their leaders to make these decisions? To say that someone who criticizes American policy is either condoning or supporting the actions of the other side is an example of the most convoluted logic. This also conveniently neglects the substance of what is being suggested.

For example, I believe that the American "negotiating" position does not offer to the other side mutual concessions and accommodations which are in line with the political realities of Vietnam. Instead of meaningful negotiations, the American position demands the total capitulation and surrender of the Viet Cong and North Vietnam. Moreover, at critical negotiating opportunities the United States has taken military actions which have stifled the negotiating atmosphere. Instead of taking cognizance of our political failures and those of our allies—French colonialism and the succession of Saigon military dictatorships—we are pursuing a military policy which can never compensate for these political failures. Escalation for a military victory is ravaging the people and land of Vietnam.

I can still recall that brisk morning in January, 1961 when I heard President Kennedy in his Inaugural Address challenge us: "So let us begin anew the quest for peace, remembering on both sides that civility is not a sign of weakness, and sincerity is always subject to proof."

In a major foreign policy speech at The American University on June 10, 1963 President Kennedy returned to this theme. "I believe that we must reexamine our own attitude [toward world peace]—as individuals and as a nation—for our attitude is as essential as theirs. . . . Every thoughtful citizen who despairs of war and wishes to bring peace, should begin by looking inward—by examining his own attitude toward the possibilities of peace."[11]

When President Kennedy asked us to look at ourselves, he did not deny the hostility and the malevolence of the other side. When I say that I believe we have fallen short in the quest for peace, I am not implying that our adversaries are either peaceful or ready to join us in the establishment of peace. When I condemn the death and destruction which pours forth from our military machine, I condemn with equal vehemence the violence of the other side.

As President Kennedy advised us, we must reexamine our own position. We must not match their intransigence with an intransigence of our own.

Senator J. William Fulbright, Chairman of the Senate Foreign Relations Committee, has succinctly expressed one of the imperatives which we who speak out have been following: "The measure of our falling short [of American ideals] is the measure of the patriot's duty of dissent."[12] The massive nature of the suffering in Vietnam has called forth an equally massive outpouring of agony by those who care for America.

If we are going to bring American practice up to American ideals, we must speak out. But I would add to Senator Fulbright's statement that our speaking out is not so much an act of dissent as it is an act of affirmation. The truth is that we are *consistently* upholding certain commitments and policies.

Diversity of opinion on how to attain the advancement of democracy is a strength in a democracy. The right to hold opinions, to settle disputes through open discussions, is the meaning of democracy.

If we abandon this right, we abandon democracy.

As I have indicated above, only certain individuals are asked to give up their rights, while others are to be left free to press their suggestions and disagreements. This is arbitrary, hypocritical, and undemocratic.

The first formal policy statement on Vietnam passed by the Senate since the Gulf of Tonkin Resolution of 1964 was adopted on March 1, 1967. The Resolution stated that

> Congress hereby declares its firm intentions to provide all necessary support for members of the armed forces of the United States fighting in Vietnam.

It also declared that Congress supports the

> efforts being made by the President of the United States and other men of goodwill throughout the world to prevent an expansion of the war in Vietnam and to bring that conflict to an end *through a negotiated settlement* which will preserve the honor of the United States, protect the vital interests of this country and allow the people of South Vietnam to determine the affairs of that nation in their own way. [Italics added.]

The Resolution passed the Senate by a vote of 72 to 19. I voted for the statement as did all of the other Senators who have sought an end to the war in line with the political realities of Vietnam. Those who voted against this statement of support for the current policy were those who have sought an increased reliance on military means to end the war.

Does this mean that those Senators should be condemned for not supporting American policy? Does this mean that they are not loyal, that they only desire to "prolong" the conflict and that they therefore should not be allowed to express dissent? Such allegations are utterly and totally false.

These are all honorable men. They disagree with the emphasis of the administration's policy. I also disagree with that policy, but for different reasons. Because we all support the United States and American fighting men, we have a right to present our opinions for the consideration of the public. In a democracy there can be no other way.

Charges and countercharges, bitterness as well as sadness permeate the public discussion of Vietnam. I hope in these pages to present facts, not accusations. My aim is not to score debating points or to indulge in recriminations—the situation is far too serious for such frivolous exercise. Rather, one of my principal hopes in writing this book is to de-escalate those aspects of the public debate on Vietnam which are a disservice to American interests, a travesty of American ideals.

We do not need recriminations, but solutions. We do not need emotional appeals, but an analysis of the facts of our involvement.

I want to help fulfill the commitments endorsed in the election of 1964.

I want to help fulfill our many solemn commitments made to the maintenance of international law and order, especially those in the Charter of the United Nations.

I want to help de-escalate the acrimonious debate on Vietnam.

I want to help put an end to death and suffering and bring our American men home.

I want to help extricate the United States I cherish and serve from *The American Crisis in Vietnam.*

I

The Roots of Struggle

Why should there be an examination of the historical background of the present struggle in Vietnam? Certainly the events that have transpired cannot be changed. What is the purpose of discussing problems that are over when there are so many problems remaining before us?

These are legitimate questions which deserve answers.

First, the present situation in Vietnam has not just emerged overnight from a *tabula rasa*. Rather, it is an outgrowth of the continuing development of Vietnam. If we are to understand what is now happening, we must view the current conflict in the context of Vietnamese history.

Second, as we are aware, the administration justifies American involvement by citing its interpretation of this past. Therefore, any assessment of the current policy must test the validity of the interpretation put forward by the administration.

Third, not only is the present course sanctioned by an analysis of the past, but also this analysis is the basis for the more important decisions of where we go from here. In terms of an analogy, the diagnosis of an ailment is the prelude to actions taken to effect a cure. Obviously, the accuracy of the original diagnosis is crucial if the right means are to be adopted so that the patient will not die.

Finally, only an understanding of the realities of Vietnam can reveal those alternatives to the current policy which will better serve as a permanent foundation for peace.

These answers suggest why we must look carefully into the past. All assumptions should be examined. If there are incorrect assumptions, an ineffective policy will be the result. This is a highly significant fact, because, as James Reston, Associate Editor of *The New York Times*, observed in January 1966, "the wrong assumptions lead to wrong decisions, and this has been the tragedy of Vietnam from the beginning."[1]

What are the wrong assumptions, the wrong interpretations in the administration's policy? These must be set aside in order to formulate the decisions for the proper future course.

By viewing the past in an objective manner, none of us is trying to cast aspersions upon the United States. As the President recently stated, "It's not required that you tear our country down and our flag down in order to lift [other nations] up."[2]

My motive is to understand the past so that we can build a better future.

Unlike the emerging countries of Africa, where nationalism is a new phenomenon, Vietnam has a long history of a people united against outside pressures. Not many nations can trace their origin as a political entity into such a distant past as can the Vietnamese. Chinese records show a visit by a prince of the Kingdom of Nam Viet to the court of Emperor Cheng in 1121 B.C.

But that first independent Vietnam on the southeastern edge of China was absorbed by the Chinese Empire in 214 B.C. or thereabouts —dates of such antiquity are often uncertain—and remained under Chinese rule for a thousand years. The Chinese left a lasting impression on the written language (Chinese was an official language well into the 20th century), on the mandarin system of education and examinations for government service, and on other culturally related areas.

Vietnamese have forgotten neither this period of Chinese dominance nor the succeeding centuries of independence, beginning in the 10th century. To be precise, it was in A.D. 939 that Ngo Quyen established national independence for Vietnam.

The Le dynasty of emperors began in 1428 with a general whose line of descendants continued to rule in Vietnam down to the late 18th century. While the size of the Vietnamese nation varied, generally it expanded toward the south. On several occasions the Emperor's forces fought off military invaders, including, in the 13th century, the redoubtable Genghis Khan and his Mongols. Tran Hung Dao, the general who turned them back, became the object of a religious cult which still exists.

But Tran Hung Dao is only one of the national heroes of the Vietnamese from long-ago centuries. In A.D. 39 the Trung Sisters organized an army and a revolt against the Chinese, resulting in four years of independence. Still heroines after 2,000 years, they were taken as a symbol by Mme. Nhu when she organized her uniformed and armed women's military corps. The anniversary of their victory even today is a national holiday in both North and South Vietnam. At least one temple in Hanoi exists in their honor, again mingling religious sentiment with patriotic history.

For more than a century and a half, beginning in 1620, control of the country was divided between the Nguyens in Saigon and the Trinh family in Hanoi, even though the Le emperors were still nominally the rulers, domiciled in Hué. In 1802, Nguyen-Anh, the southern or Cochin China ruler, toppled the northerners and again united Vietnam as Emperor Gia Long, with his palace in Hué. That modern period of national unity lasted nearly sixty years.

The period of French domination began no longer ago than our own Civil War; and I suspect that some Americans' nostalgia for an antebellum South has its counterpart among Vietnamese who look back to a united nation under its own leadership such as they had before the fall of Saigon, after a year's siege, in 1861. With the exception of the Japanese interlude during World War II, when the Vichy government cooperated with Japanese occupation forces in Indo-China, France dominated Vietnam until 1954.

Unfortunately, the United States strongly supported the postwar French colonial policy. From 1950 to 1954, the United States paid 80 per cent of the costs of the French colonialist war fought to prevent the Vietnamese from gaining their independence. French policy was aligned completely against the long history of Vietnamese nationalism. Given the strength of this Vietnamese feeling, the end of French colonial rule was only a matter of time.

Professor Frank N. Trager in his recent book *Why Viet Nam?* demonstrated that he is a supporter of the current administration's policy. Therefore, his judgment on American policy cannot be dismissed as that of a "cusser and doubter." His analysis (in an earlier book) of the first extensive contact by the Vietnamese people with the United States is extremely important:

> Throughout the long devastating years from the postwar return of the French in Indo-China to Dien Bien Phu, the United States supported with incredible consistency the imperialist aims of France in Indo-China.[3]

Under France, Cochin China—southernmost of the three areas into which Vietnam was divided by the French—was an outright colony. There, in Saigon and outside the capital as well, all government posts—even down to police and postmen—were filled by French. In the central portion, Annam, the throne at Hué was still occupied by an emperor, but the government staffed by Vietnamese civil servants was paralleled by a French structure keeping tight rein on the processes of government. In northern Tonkin, also a "protectorate" and nominally under the Emperor, the French officials at Hanoi ran affairs with even less pretense of joint rule. The Emperor and the court, in fact, with tax collection in French hands, were dependent on allotments from the French authorities. Over all of the five-part Union of Indo-China, which also embraced Cambodia and Laos, was the French Governor General, aided by "Résidents Supérieurs."

"Vietnamese independence had come to an end," says a political-science text on Southeast Asia, "but Vietnamese resistance to French rule, in both the north and south, continued into the twentieth century."[4] Armed opposition, led by high-ranking mandarins and members of the imperial family, in fact continued until 1916.[5]

Hatred for the French was described in 1947 by an American observer as "a living, leaping thing in the land. You read it in the faces of the ordinary people. . . . It was like a social disease of the subjected, this passionate loathing. Whole generations had been infected with it, by the vermin in French prisons or by the slower poison of an enforced inferiority haunting every step of their lives from cradle to grave."[6] Although thwarted, nationalism could not be stamped out.

Political imprisonment for anti-French activity held an estimated 10,000 in the prisons of Vietnam in 1932, according to one estimate; of nearly 3,000 political arrests in 1930, 86 resulted in a death sentence.[7] The suppression of educational advantages was one of the means to "enforced inferiority": under French rule there were only fourteen secondary schools in all of Vietnam, and only 1 per cent of the half-million who had attended elementary schools were able to reach secondary schools in 1939. At that time the only university, founded at Hanoi in 1917, had only 631 students[8]—this for a population as great as present-day New York State and Michigan combined. Those few who secured an education in France often returned to lead in anti-French activity.

The opportunities to expand the anti-French struggle were greatly facilitated by the disruption during World War II. Because of the war, complete French control ended, although there was a dual French-Japanese administration.

In the forefront of the fight against the French was the Revolutionary League for the Independence of Vietnam (Viet Nam Doc Lap Dong Minh). This united front organization was dominated by the Communists, but it also included a wide variety of non-Communist nationalists. Ho Chi Minh, the acknowledged leader of the Viet Minh, stated that their aim was "to unite all patriots, without distinction of fortune, age, sex, religion or political opinions, to work together for the liberation of our people and the salvation of our nation."[9]

I find it extremely unfortunate and lamentable that the leaders of the movement for independence were Ho Chi Minh and the Communist-dominated Viet Minh. However, for the purposes of American policy, we must pay particular attention to the significant ramifications of these developments.

Because they were working against the Japanese, the Viet Minh were able to advance their own cause by securing the cooperation of the Allies. For example, Ho was paid by the Chinese Nationalists for collecting intelligence information in Vietnam. Later on, the American Office of Strategic Services provided assistance to Ho's organization in return for underground operations against the Japanese.

Of course, while Ho and the Viet Minh were laboring with the assistance of the Allies, they were also advancing their own interests. They were able to organize Vietnamese nationalism and build their strength at many levels of society.

As a result of these actions, the Viet Minh fell heir to the claim of being the legitimate leaders of the struggle for independence. They attracted to their side many non-Communists who desired to free Vietnam from French colonialism. The Viet Minh were also respected and looked up to by the peasants.

Finally we must not overlook the fact that the predominance of Ho Chi Minh and the Viet Minh was partially a function of the absence of any genuine, popular non-Communist movement. The only alternative available to the people of Vietnam was to support either the Viet Minh or the hated French.

The swift termination of World War II in the Pacific left a power vacuum in Vietnam. The Japanese were defeated. The former colonial masters, the French, did not immediately have the power to reassert their command.

The Viet Minh rapidly moved into the vacuum in order to establish a nationalist, independent government for Vietnam. Hanoi was taken from the Japanese on August 19, Hué on August 23, and Saigon on August 25. The whole of Vietnam was reunited under the government of the Democratic Republic of Vietnam with Ho Chi Minh as its leader.

On August 22 the emperor, Bao Dai, wrote to General De Gaulle as the new head of France, asking him "to recognize frankly the independence of Viet-Nam and to renounce any idea of reestablishing French sovereignty or administration here." Writing the day before Hanoi's capture by the Viet Minh, while the Japanese still held Hué, Bao Dai told De Gaulle that a French administration "would no longer be obeyed; each village would be a nest of resistance, every former friend an enemy, and your officials and colonists themselves would ask to depart from this unbreathable atmosphere."[10]

Bao Dai, who had continued as emperor under Vichy, on August 26 handed over the gold seal of office and the gold sword with ruby-encrusted handle, abdicating to become Citizen Vinh Thuy. Ho Chi Minh made him "Supreme Advisor" to the new republic. On September 2, before a crowd of 500,000 in Hanoi, Ho Chi Minh read the Vietnamese Declaration of Independence he had prepared.

Its first words were those of our own Declaration: "All men are created equal. They are endowed by their Creator with certain unalienable rights. Among these are life, liberty, and the pursuit of happiness." This "immortal statement" was followed by a quotation from the French Revolution's 1791 Declaration of the Rights of Man. A list of grievances and oppressions was set forth, and the achievement of independence was affirmed. Near the end comes this sentence: "We are convinced that the Allied nations which have acknowledged at Teheran and San Francisco the principles of self-determination and equality of status will not refuse to acknowledge the independence of Viet-nam."[11]

This was not the first occasion on which Ho had made an appeal to Western principles on behalf of Vietnamese rights. On the basis of the ideals enunciated by President Woodrow Wilson, in 1919 Ho signed a Vietnamese appeal written to the Allied leaders gathered at Versailles. These Vietnamese asked for the independence of Vietnam in accordance with the principle of national self-determination enunciated by the Allies. Like the hope of 1945 expressed by all Vietnamese—not just Ho—for independence, this earlier appeal was summarily rejected.

The Vietnamese Declaration of Independence of 1945 also referred to the strong and long standing pride of Vietnamese nationalism which has been touched upon above: "Our people have broken the chains which for nearly a century have fettered them and have won independence for the Fatherland."

The evidence reveals that there was a genuine desire among all Vietnamese for the termination of French imperialism and for the independence of their country. As the letter of Emperor Bao Dai exemplifies, both Communists and non-Communists demanded independence. For our purposes we must not forget the fact that the Communists were the principal organized group leading the struggle for independence.

There was an enthusiastic welcome for the establishment of the Democratic Republic of Vietnam by Vietnamese from all parts of the country. The administrative offices of Cochin China in Saigon were taken over swiftly and peaceably by the Committee of the South, an extension of the Hanoi leadership. But it was to sit in the seats of the former French rulers for less than a month, when the country would again be divided.

To understand how the North-South split began and grew to today's war, it is necessary to move into the realm of postwar Western politics.

At Potsdam, anticipating the end of the war, it was agreed that for purposes of transferring authority from the Japanese to the Allies, the Vietnam area would be divided at the 16th parallel. North of that line the Chinese would restore order, while in the South the British would be in charge. While the Vietnamese were thinking in terms of independence, the Allies were not.

The Japanese forces were under Allied orders to keep the peace until an Allied army of occupation arrived. Twenty thousand French civilians in Saigon waited eagerly for the occupation forces, hoping for restoration of French dominance if not actual rule.

The Committee of the South, however, believed that, in the words of Ellen Hammer's definitive study, "the Vietnamese had only to convince the United Nations of their ability to rule themselves, and their independence would be recognized by the world."[12] They urged cooperation by the Vietnamese, no reprisals against the French, and even declared that anyone inciting the people to arm themselves would be treated as a saboteur. There was need to show the Allies a stable order.

But on September 2, the day of Ho Chi Minh's Declaration in Hanoi, the peace was broken during a mass demonstration in Saigon. A French priest known as a friend of the Vietnamese was shot and killed at the cathedral doorway as the crowds were assembling there. There were other shots, and both Vietnamese and French were wounded, two killed. Looting and disorder followed. French fears intensified as French–Vietnamese tensions grew.

It was a long ten days before the British and Indian forces under Major General Douglas Gracey arrived in Saigon by air from Rangoon, to be greeted by banners both of welcome to them and of bitterness toward the French. Their force was so small that they had to rely on Japanese patrols to keep order.

General Gracey was under instructions to stick to his military assignment, but before leaving India he had said, "Civil and military control of Indochina by the French is only a question of weeks."[13] He forbade the Vietnamese press to publish, imposed a curfew, proclaimed martial law, banned all demonstrations and public meetings. Repeated protests by the governing Committee of the South were ignored.

The fate of the Committee, and with it of Vietnamese independence in the South, was sealed with the *coup d'état* carried out by the French under Colonel Cedile in the early morning of September 23, 1945. A thousand men, drawn from the barracks of the Vichy force, were selected and given arms. These "ragged soldiers," with another 500 paratroopers recently arrived from France, made arrests and took over the government headquarters, post office, and police headquarters. Saigon's participation in Ho Chi Minh's reunited Vietnam had lasted less than a month.

The French population "went wild; they insulted and attacked any Vietnamese who dared appear on the streets, while French and British soldiers looked on."[14] General Gracey now invited the previously ignored Vietnamese leaders of the Committee to come in for negotiations with the French under his auspices.

The orders of General Gracey had been explicit: "Sole mission: disarm the Japanese. Do not get involved in keeping order." The General wrote of his experience, "I was welcomed on arrival by Viet Minh, who said 'welcome' and all that sort of thing. It was a very unpleasant situation and I promptly kicked them out."[15]

There followed a general strike, attacks and atrocities by Vietnamese, a blockade of Saigon. It was unsafe for French residents to go out alone. The American OSS chief in Saigon was killed, apparently mistaken for French. Finally a British warship arrived at the end of the month. Vietnamese fled to the countryside. Before Christmas, 1945, there were 50,000 French troops in the southern zone, and the British prepared to withdraw. "We have done our best for the French," General Gracey told an American, Harold Isaacs.[16] Nehru, struggling for Indian independence, denounced the use of Indian troops "for doing Britain's dirty work against our friends who are fighting the same fight as we."

By early 1946, French troops held the Cochin China cities, and the rubber plantations were in French hands again. But outside the areas of control they could move only in convoys. Guerrilla war had begun in the South, war against the return of colonialism.

In the North, above the 16th parallel, the Chinese were in the same relative position as the British in the South. The Yalta Conference had granted Manchurian territory to Russia; the subsequent Potsdam authority for Chiang Kai-shek to occupy Indo-China down to the 16th parallel was a recognition both of this loss and of Chinese "interest" in the area.

Chinese occupation troops arrived in September, but their attitude toward the new regime did not follow that of the pro-French British. Vietnamese were permitted to keep their weapons, but Frenchmen in Hanoi were disarmed and any arriving French searched for arms. French requests to bring in soldiers and civil administrators fell on deaf ears; government buildings and administration were left to the Viet Minh leaders. Carrying out their occupation duties, the Chinese forces disarmed the Japanese and concentrated them along the coast to await repatriation ships to take them home. They dismantled French fortifications on the Chinese frontier. The result was, in the North, a consolidation rather than a disruption of the Democratic Republic of Vietnam.

In order to continue as a viable government, it was obvious that Hanoi would have to come to some sort of understanding with the French. The recognition of the *de facto* independence of the D.R.V. came in a remarkable document signed at Hanoi on March 6, 1946. "The French government," says the agreement, "recognizes the Republic of Vietnam as a free state, having its own government, parliament, army and treasury, belonging to the Indo-Chinese Federation and to the French Union."[17]

In return, Ho Chi Minh agreed to replacement of the Chinese forces by 15,000 French troops, to be assisted by 10,000 Vietnamese under their command. The French further agreed to abide by a referendum concerning unification of Tonkin, Annam, and Cochin China; to withdraw units guarding Japanese prisoners "as soon as their mission is completed"—within ten months; and to replace one-fifth of their other troops with Vietnamese each year, thus completing military withdrawal in five years. Further negotiations with Ho Chi Minh in Paris during the late summer led to another amicable agreement, signed in September, spelling out details of the new coexistence.

In the South, where Cochin China was now counted by the French as, in effect, a restored colony, French-Vietnamese conflict continued. By March 6, according to General Leclerc months later, some 1,200 French had been killed in Indo-China, and the Vietnamese toll was much greater. Yet on March 18 Leclerc's troops landing in Hanoi were welcomed by the Vietnamese, although many were skeptical of Ho Chi Minh's agreement. In October the second National Assembly met. Five political parties held seats, with Viet Minh members accounting for the largest number, 80—but there were also 90 unaffiliated independents. However, Ho Chi Minh's new cabinet took on a dominant Communist complexion. Not only were there five ministries held by Communists, but in the others the non-Communist ministers had Communist deputies.

But hopes for *rapprochement* between France and the government of Ho Chi Minh, even as negotiations continued that summer, became dimmer. The French were demonstrating a complete intransigence in their refusal to deal with the Vietnamese amicably on the basis of the March 6 agreement. There were increasingly frequent clashes. Vietnamese of a less patient turn saw little virtue in collaboration with the French, who to them appeared bent on returning the North to colonial status as they had done in Saigon. In November, an incident at Haiphong concerning a French patrol boat led to shelling by a heavy cruiser[18] in which 6,000 Vietnamese were killed.

The French continued to violate their signed agreements.

On December 19, 1946 General Morliere, the French commander, demanded that the Viet Minh militia disarm. That night the Vietnamese turned on the French in Hanoi, cutting off water and electricity, and attacked with machine guns, mortars, and artillery. From Hanoi the fighting spread rapidly throughout the North, down into the former Annam, and was followed by renewed attacks on the French in the South. French forces occupied Hanoi and in the repression following the December 19 clash several thousand Vietnamese civilians lost their lives. Efforts at cooperation with Vietnamese in the North were completely ended. The "First Indo-Chinese War" had begun.

Ellen Hammer has offered this well-reasoned conclusion on the causes of the outbreak of this war:

> The Vietnamese chose the date on which it broke out, but the policy followed by members of the French administration in Saigon made the war almost inevitable. They had systematically obstructed the carrying out of the March 6 agreement.[19]

II

Two Vietnams—
and American Involvement

The pictures in *Life* show a gaunt Vietnamese woman clutching her child in the doorway of her home; troops in battle gear fording a stream, weapons held high; a half-clad young prisoner, hands behind his back, being interrogated by his uniformed captor. The article they illustrate is titled "The Saddest War."

But the captions dispel any quick conclusion that this is current history. The husband of the "Annamite woman" is "off fighting the French colonial troops"; French, not Americans, are fording the river, fighting "in the sweating jungles and rice paddies," and losing 600 men a month. The prisoner is a "Vietnamese partisan," not a Viet Cong, and his questioner is a French Foreign Legionnaire. The date is December 29, 1947, and the author of the article the former Ambassador to France and to Russia, William C. Bullitt.

Mr. Bullitt acknowledges that "Not one in a hundred Annamites is a Communist, but all decent Annamites want independence." He reports that "no other living Annamite has such personal prestige" as Ho Chi Minh. Most Annamites regard him "as the father of his country." But the dilemma is that he is a Communist.

The 115,000 French troops are inadequate, badly equipped; at least 500,000 "would be needed to reconquer" Vietnam. There are unhappy nationalists who are not Communists, and France should come to terms with them on the future of the country so they can help the French as guerrillas "for the elimination of the Communists."[1]

The French were well aware of their need to win over non-Communist Vietnamese nationalists. But the cooperative government in Cochin China was looked upon by those who disliked Ho Chi Minh's views as distastefully collaborationist; the "president" of the regime in the South was then Nguyen Van Xuan, a brigadier general (and the first Vietnamese to gain that rank) in the French army.

In casting about for a solution, the French were already considering Bao Dai—still nominally "Supreme Advisor" to the Viet Minh government, but in Hong Kong since March—particularly since various pro-Bao Dai groups had been formed among Vietnamese on the French side. Bullitt had just visited Bao Dai in Hong Kong, and his article was taken as more or less official American endorsement of him. About the time of the Bullitt article, Bao Dai left for Europe for talks with the French government.

During the same period, Ho Chi Minh was still trying to persuade the French to live up to the terms of the March 6, 1946 agreement. He had left behind a delegation in France after signing the September 14, 1946 *modus vivendi* agreement. In February 1947 this delegation proposed a cease-fire, the appointment of an armistice commission, and negotiations with the Ho Chi Minh "legal government" on the basis of the March and September accords. A poll of French opinion announced the same month showed 42 per cent favoring negotiations, 8 per cent in favor of France leaving Vietnam entirely. Against that 50 per cent, there were 14 per cent with no opinion and 36 per cent in favor of force.[2]

Within the French government, too, there were critics of military action instead of negotiation. But Premier Ramadier refused to accept the March 6, 1946 agreement which he said had been broken by "the aggression of Hanoi"—a phrase with a familiar ring to Americans twenty years later.[3] The March 6 agreement, it will be recalled, was the one in which the French government "recognizes the Republic of Vietnam as a free state . . . belonging to the Indo-Chinese Federation and to the French Union."[4] It continued to be the basis for Ho Chi Minh's claims.

On March 1, 1947 Ho Chi Minh himself appealed to the French government and people, declaring that "the Vietnamese people desire only unity and independence in the French Union, and we pledge ourselves to respect French economic and cultural interests."[5] "If France would but say the word to cease hostilities immediately," he said, "so many lives and so much property would be saved. . . ."[6]

Again in March, the foreign minister of the D.R.V. made the same offer: ". . . the Vietnamese Government proposes to the French Government the immediate cessation of hostilities and the opening of negotiations for a peaceful settlement of the conflict." In April, the Vietnamese once more asked for an armistice, and this time the new High Commissioner in Saigon, Emile Bollaert, sent a distinguished emissary to see Ho Chi Minh. But the offer Paul Mus brought—and again it sounds like history rehearsing—was for a cease-fire on terms "amounting to unconditional surrender." Reaching Ho's headquarters after a six-mile march on foot, Mus, who had been given no negotiating authority, had to admit to Ho Chi Minh that if he were in Ho's place he would not accept such terms.[7]

In August 1947 a Viet Minh spokesman told the French Minister in Bangkok that Ho Chi Minh would accept unity and independence within the French Union, with close cultural and economic collaboration—essentially what the March 6, 1946 agreement had specified. But he went further. The French, he said, could have bases at six specified places, two of which have names familiar to Americans today—Cam Ranh and Danang.° The French press reported it only months later.[8]

The Viet Minh government did not stop with appeals to France. A letter went to United Nations Secretary General Trygve Lie, signed by the Undersecretary of State of the D.R.V. and dated September 12, 1947. Dr. Pham Ngoc Thach asked that the Security Council "put an end to the war of aggression that France has undertaken these last two years against Viet Nam." He proposed peace negotiations between Vietnam and France "under the auspices and guarantee of the United Nations." There was no reply.[9]

More than a year later, on October 27, 1948, Ho Chi Minh's Paris spokesman was still setting forth Vietnamese willingness to negotiate for peace, reaffirming readiness to cooperate "within the framework of the [French] Union and . . . of the United Nations."[10]

Another effort by the government of Ho Chi Minh to find a way out of the impasse with France was its application for membership in the United Nations, dated November 22, 1948. In it, reference was made to existence of the government "as an independent sovereign state" since September 2, 1945, the date of the Declaration of Independence, and to French recognition by the March 6, 1946 agreement.

In the meantime, the French efforts to build a new opposition state around Bao Dai had been continuing.[11] The ex-Emperor had value to the French if he could split away Vietnamese from Ho Chi Minh. But he

°   *Then called Tourane most generally.*

could hope to do this only by being an anti-French nationalist. So he held out against French blandishments which failed to satisfy nationalism for the non-Communists, and negotiations dragged on, until finally the Elysée Accords of March 8, 1949 were signed. Bao Dai came back to Vietnam, acting as though he had never abdicated. On June 14 he declared himself Chief of State, retaining the title of Emperor "in order to have a legal international position" until the people could decide their own future constitution. With French backing, he claimed the same territory—all of Vietnam—which was covered by the agreement of March 6 three years earlier with Ho Chi Minh.

With the appearance of the Bao Dai government, it would seem that there were now two Vietnams, one government in Hanoi and one at Saigon. However, such a superficial description could not accurately reflect the realities in Vietnam.

In the first place, the war against the Viet Minh was never prosecuted by the Bao Dai "government" but by the French army. Bao Dai was accurately viewed as a French puppet, a representative of French imperialism. He was not looked upon by the Vietnamese people as a Vietnamese alternative to the D.R.V. The non-Communist, nationalist Dr. Phan Quang Dan observed that "what they called a Bao Dai solution turned out to be just a French solution."[12] Robert Blum, who was Chief of Mission for the U.S. Special Mission to Vietnam from April 1950 to November 1951, drew the same conclusion from his experiences. Writing in 1951, he said that "the Bao Dai government gives little promise of developing competence and winning the loyalty of the population."[13]

Secondly, Vietnam was seen as one by the majority of the people with its acknowledged leader Ho Chi Minh. The artificiality of "two" Vietnams in the eyes of Vietnamese was again demonstrated much more recently in a public opinion survey of Vietnamese conducted for the Columbia Broadcasting System in December 1966 and January 1967. Results showed that 83 per cent of the South Vietnamese people "want reunification very much."[14]

In the absence of a *Vietnamese,* non-Communist alternative, the Viet Minh, then, rather than the Saigon government came to be looked upon as the prime movers for independence. "The Communists," Theodore Draper concludes, "maneuvered themselves into increasingly advantageous positions precisely because the French administration was hostile to Vietnamese nationalism."[15] Similarly, Robert Shaplen speaks of the "ardent nationalists who . . . gravitated naturally to the Viet-Minh because it was the most active dynamic center of attraction."[16]

It was unfortunate that this course of events transpired. But regardless of our approval or disapproval, the fact facing us is that the Communists were seen as the genuine leaders of the movement for independence. All of us would have preferred a different outcome. However, the importance of examining the past is to be able to see clearly the significance which these developments hold for the future.

If the turn of events in the struggle for independence was unfortunate, then the manner in which the United States reacted was even more tragic.

Although the United States was granting large amounts of assistance to France under NATO agreements and the Marshall Plan, the first formal announcement of military aid for Indo-China was made in May 1950. The qualifications put upon this aid are important:

> The problem of meeting the threat to the security of Vietnam, Cambodia, and Laos which now enjoy independence within the French Union is *primarily the responsibility of France and the Governments and peoples of Indochina*. The United States recognizes that the solution to the Indochina problem depends upon the restoration of security and upon the *development of genuine nationalism*.[17]

On May 30 a U.S. economic mission arrived in Saigon, and on June 27, two days after the Korean War began with action spearheaded by Russian-built tanks, President Truman announced that he had "directed acceleration in the furnishing of military assistance to the forces of France and the Associated States in Indochina and the dispatch of a military mission to provide close working relations with those forces."[18]

The opportunity to work for "the development of genuine nationalism" was pushed into the background because of the military emphasis in American policy associated with the Korean War. Edmund Gullion, the U.S. Chargé d'Affaires in Vietnam, felt that the United States should have used her power to get the French to live up to their agreements to grant the Vietnamese more freedom. He wrote that "we really should have pushed the French after the Elysee agreements of March, 1949. . . . But then we got involved in Korea, and since the French were in trouble in Indochina, we pulled our punches."[19] Theodore Draper has also observed that "The American decision to support the French was all the more incongruous in view of the fact that, at this very time, the United States was urging, if not pressing, the British to get out of India and Burma and the Dutch to give up Indonesia."[20]

The military mission arrived in Saigon on July 15, 1950 and the first U.S. war materials were landed on August 10. On August 16, Ho Chi

25

48789

LIBRARY
College of St. Francis
JOLIET, ILL.

Minh spoke over the Viet Minh radio. "Since the beginning of the war," he said, "the Americans have tried to help the French bandits. But now they have advanced one more step to direct intervention in Vietnam. Thus, we now have one principal opponent—the French bandits—and one more opponent—the American interventionists."[21]

Since the beginning of the Marshall Plan, American dollars poured into the French economy had released billions of francs for the war in Vietnam, which cost 102 billion francs ($291,000,000) in 1946 and rose to 177 billion (over $500,000,000) in 1949.[22] Specific U.S. aid and loans "for military use in Indo-China" were already $400,000,000 in 1948, and more than $750,000,000 in 1949. The total for Vietnam military operations, supplied by the United States, exceeded $2 billion by the end of 1951, and by the end of 1954 it was over $4 billion. In the last stages of the French effort, before the fall of Dien Bien Phu on May 8, 1954, the United States was paying the bill for 80 per cent of the French cost.[23] In addition, we had assisted France with another $7.5 billion primarily for her own military and the French NATO forces. Some of this money undoubtedly was diverted to Indo-China although earmarked for Europe.[24]

How did this American involvement on behalf of the French colonialist war appear to the Vietnamese people? Robert Blum has made the harsh but accurate judgment that "we came to be looked upon more as a supporter of colonialism than as a friend of the new nation."[25] Because of this support of French colonialism and the parallel neglect of the "development of genuine nationalism" of the Vietnamese people, Shaplen concludes that:

> the chance was lost . . . between the years 1948 and 1953, to create, in the southern part of Vietnam, a challenging alternative to the emerging Communism in the north.[26]

The French people, as I have noted, had no enthusiasm for *la guerre pourrie* ("the rotten war") which cost the lives of 72,200 of their forces during its nine years. Seventy-two per cent of those losses, however, were not among mainland French, who were in a distinct minority. 26,666 were Vietnamese dead; 15,229 had come from French Africa; and 11,620 were soldiers of the French Foreign Legion, many of whose members in the immediate postwar period were ex-German members of the *Wehrmacht* who joined up after their defeat.[27] There is one very significant fact about the French conduct of the *guerre pourrie* that is not generally known: Not one French draftee ever fought in Vietnam.

A prominent member of an inter-religious clergy team which undertook a personal mission of investigation in Southeast Asia in the summer of 1965 has commented on the contrast with our own position today. Dr. Howard Schomer, President of Chicago Theological Seminary, lived and taught in France and French Switzerland from 1946 to 1958, seeing the French reaction from the inside. In an address at Dubuque University on February 4, 1966, he said this:

> *No French prime minister ever dared to send a single draftee from mainland France to fight in Indochina.*
> For under the French Constitution this could not be done by mere executive order, and . . . this "First Indochinese War" was so profoundly *unpopular* in France that any government which had attempted to send French draftees to fight in Vietnam would surely have been overthrown in the National Assembly. . . .
> What a sharp contrast with the readiness with which many Americans today rubber-stamp this "Second Indochinese War," which they have trouble locating on the map, don't know how their country got into and wouldn't claim to understand! For an American who lived in France throughout that "First Indochinese War," it is simply unbelievable that the American public has, almost without congressional debate, allowed the Eisenhower, Kennedy and Johnson administrations gradually to commit billions of dollars and several hundred thousand men to an open-ended land-war in Asia, with only clichés for objectives and twelve years of miscalculated predictions as proof of feasibility.[28]

Despite these facts, the American "commitment" has time and again, and most officially, been presented to the nation as dating not from the discredited Bao Dai period but from the beginning of the Diem regime and the time of the Geneva Accords. Perhaps the foremost official document dealing with this question is the 27-page brochure issued under the title *Why Vietnam*, with a foreword by President Johnson, dated August 20, 1965.[29]

The first section of this apologia is titled "The Roots of Commitment," beginning with the text of a letter of April 4, 1954 addressed to "Dear Winston" and signed "Ike," and followed by another Eisenhower letter of October 1, 1954 to President Diem. There are no earlier "roots of commitment" mentioned.

Next, President Johnson in a July 28, 1965 statement reprinted in *Why Vietnam* says, likewise as though there were no previous history: "Moreover, we are in Vietnam to fulfill one of the most solemn pledges of the American Nation. Three Presidents—President Eisenhower, President Kennedy, and your President—over 11 years, have committed themselves and have promised to help defend this small and valiant nation. . . ." The clear implication is that the American involvement began under Eisenhower.

Testimony by Secretary Rusk is reprinted from an August 3, 1965 appearance before the House Foreign Affairs Committee. In a section headed "The Commitment," he unequivocally puts its beginnings in the framework of SEATO: "Let us be clear about our commitment in Vietnam. It began with the Southeast Asia Treaty, which was negotiated and signed after the Geneva agreements and the ceasefire in Indo-China in 1954 and was approved by the United States Senate by a vote of 82 to 1 in February 1955." No date prior to 1954 is mentioned.

Perhaps Secretary Rusk is making a fine distinction between the early "involvement" and the post-Geneva "commitment." But if so, one can only ask why, if we had no earlier "commitment," did we pour out those thousands of millions before the French defeat at Dien Bien Phu?

Obviously, no one wants to claim this legacy of American support for French colonialism. But the truth is that this involvement was the first in a steady succession of "wrong assumptions" which produced "wrong decisions." This involvement would only be the first of many occasions when we would try to reverse political failures by taking a ride on the military escalator. As Senator Richard B. Russell of Georgia has stated, "we have made every conceivable blunder" in Vietnam.[30]

This colonialist legacy, the ability of the Communists to stand in the forefront of the nationalist movement, and the absence of a non-Communist Vietnamese alternative truly are a grim burden for American policy. But these years were only the beginning of the unhappy situation which Dennis Warner has aptly described: "The tyranny the West allied with in Saigon was in many ways worse than the tyranny it was fighting against."[31]

Now let us turn from our "involvement" to an examination of our "commitment" which carries us deeper and deeper into the morass.

III

The Nature of Our Commitment

The French-American effort to maintain colonial rule in Vietnam is obviously far too embarrassing to be included in our "commitment" to Vietnam. How valid are the other "commitments" which the administration constantly refers to as being the basis of the current policy? Let us carefully examine the facts to determine exactly what is the nature of our commitment in Vietnam.

The letter of October 23, 1954 from President Eisenhower to Ngo Dinh Diem, as we have said, is generally cited as the first American commitment to Vietnam. Because of this letter, according to the argument of the administration, we must follow the present course in Vietnam in order to demonstrate that "America keeps her word." What was the exact nature of the word given by America? Has the United States kept that word?

The first paragraph of the Eisenhower letter—there are four—is a general expression of "interest" and "grave concern" for the future of a country "temporarily divided by an artificial military grouping" and weak from the long war just concluded. It is sympathetic but it carries no word of commitment.

The second paragraph says that "your recent requests for aid" in resettling refugees from the North "are being fulfilled." The President is glad we can "assist in this humanitarian effort," but makes no commitment to any military effort.

The last two paragraphs contain the terms under which the proposed aid would be granted. They are important enough to be read by all Americans and deserve inclusion in full.

> We have been exploring ways and means to permit our aid to Vietnam to be more effective and to make a greater contribution to the welfare and stability of the Government of Vietnam. I am, accordingly, instructing the American Ambassador to Vietnam to examine with you in your capacity as Chief of Government, how an intelligent program of American aid given directly to your Government can serve to assist Vietnam in its present hour of trial, *provided that your Government is prepared to give assurances as to the standards of performance it would be able to maintain in the event such aid were supplied.*
>
> The purpose of this offer is to assist the Government of Vietnam in developing and maintaining a strong, viable state, capable of resisting attempted subversion or aggression through military means. The Government of the United States *expects that this aid will be met by performance on the part of the Government of Vietnam in undertaking needed reforms.* It hopes that such aid, *combined with your own continuing efforts,* will contribute effectively toward an independent Vietnam endowed with a strong Government. Such a Government would, I hope, be so responsive to the nationalist aspirations of its people, so enlightened in purpose and effective in performance, that it will be respected both at home and abroad and discourage any who might wish to impose a foreign ideology on your free people.[1]

No generalization, no analogy, no charge or statement of mine could ever refute the contention of the administration as completely as do these words of President Eisenhower. This letter is a direct contradiction to the administration's case that the Eisenhower letter is a justification of the current policy.

There is no unilateral commitment of American honor made to the Diem regime in this letter. There is not even an unqualified promise of American economic aid, let alone anything which could possibly be construed as a promise of American soldiers. President Eisenhower himself stated on August 17, 1965 that the letter was meant as an offer of economic, not military, aid.[2]

This letter is not a blank check. It is not a commitment of American honor to the Diem regime. In its diplomatic language and approach, it is a demand for reforms by the Vietnamese.

These reforms were not carried out by Diem or by the succession of Saigon regimes. The Honorable Chester Bowles, Ambassador to India, recently described the implications of the failure to carry out these reforms:

> The team of American specialists who sparked the agrarian reforms in Japan, Taiwan, and South Korea made a similar effort in South Vietnam in the mid-1950's. However, reactionary forces in the Diem Government and lack of strong support from the United States blocked the necessary changes.
>
> If this effort had succeeded, it is unlikely that American troops would now be involved in this tragic country, fighting against peasant guerrillas.[3]

As the performance of the Government of Vietnam plummeted, the American commitment, contrary to the Eisenhower letter, vastly increased.

America did give her word, but not in the way the administration suggests. In line with our finest ideals and achievements, the letter of President Eisenhower said that we would assist a government that was ready to help her people. Tragically, America has not kept that word.

President Johnson said in the State of the Union message of January 12, 1966, as on other occasions, "We fight for the principle of self-determination. . . . The people of all Vietnam should make a free decision on the great question of reunification. . . . We stand by the Geneva Agreements. . . ."

The Geneva Conference produced two major documents dealing with Vietnam. One, the "Agreement on the Cessation of Hostilities," was signed for the contending armies by a French general and Ho Chi Minh's Vice Minister of National Defense. The other, the "Final Declaration of the Geneva Conference," was not actually signed by anyone. Instead, at the closing plenary session, Chairman Anthony Eden asked each of the nine delegation heads for comments. Eight of them gave verbal assent; the United States, represented by Under Secretary of State Walter Bedell Smith, made a "unilateral declaration of its position."[4]

"America keeps her word." What was the exact nature of the word given by America? Has the United States kept that word?

The Declaration of Geneva never intended to make the 17th parallel the permanent dividing line between two separate and independent countries. It says that "the military demarcation line is provisional and should not in any way be interpreted as constituting a political or territorial boundary." It further says that "general elections shall be held in July, 1956, under the supervision of an international commission. . . . Consultations will be held on this subject between the competent representative authorities of the two zones from July 20, 1955." Vietnam was considered a single entity, temporarily divided for purposes of the cease-fire, to be reunited by an internationally supervised election.

We very specifically endorsed that view. The words of Mr. Smith in our "unilateral declaration" are worth quoting:

> The Government of the United States being resolved to devote its efforts to the strengthening of peace in accordance with the principles and purposes of the United Nations
> *Takes note* of the Agreements concluded at Geneva. . .
> *Declares* with regard to the aforesaid Agreements and paragraphs that (i) it will refrain from the threat or the use of force to disturb them in accordance with . . . the Charter of the United Nations . . .; and (ii) it would view any renewal of the aggression in violation of the aforesaid Agreements with grave concern and as seriously threatening international peace and security.
> In connexion with the statement in the Declaration concerning free elections in Vietnam, my Government wishes to make clear its position which it has expressed in a Declaration made in Washington on June 29, 1954* as follows:
> "In the case of nations now divided against their will, we shall continue to seek to achieve unity through free elections, supervised by the United Nations to ensure that they are conducted fairly."
> With respect to the statement made by the Representative of the State of Vietnam, *the United States reiterates its traditional position that peoples are entitled to determine their own future and that it will not join in an arrangement which would hinder this.* Nothing in its declaration just made is intended to or does indicate any departure from this traditional position. [Italics added.]

On July 19, 1955, the D.R.V. sent a letter to the Diem government asking for a meeting of the pre-election consultative conference scheduled by the Geneva Agreements to begin July 20, 1955. The South Vietnamese government refused even to discuss the possibility of holding the election of July 1956 which was called for in Article 14 of the

---

* *This was the joint Eisenhower-Churchill "Potomac Declaration."*

"Agreement on the Cessation of Hostilities" and in Article 7 of the "Final Declaration."

On January 28, 1966, Chairman Fulbright asked Secretary Rusk "why in 1956, contrary to the terms of the Geneva accords, elections were not held." In the course of his response the Secretary said, "Well, neither his [Diem's] government nor the Government of the United States signed that agreement."[5]

This answer contradicts the spirit of the Geneva agreements, contradicts the position of the United States given by Mr. Bedell Smith on the Geneva Agreements, and is not even technically accurate, since the Bao Dai-Diem government was the successor to the French Union Forces which did sign the Cessation Agreement. As quoted above, Article 14 of that signed document called for a general election for reunification, as did article 7 of the Declaration.

Who was responsible for the failure to hold the scheduled elections on reunification in July 1956? The Sixth Interim Report of the International Commission for Supervision and Control in Vietnam (covering activities for the year 1956) registered this conclusion:

> Neither party has fulfilled in their entirety these obligations. As has been revealed in the preceding paragraphs, the degree of cooperation given to the Commission by the two parties has not been the same. While the Commission has experienced difficulties in North Vietnam, the *major part of its difficulties has arisen in South Vietnam.*[6] [Italics added.]

Why were the elections not held? The answer to this question is quite clear. As President Eisenhower confided in his memoirs, everyone believed that "had elections been held as of the time of the fighting, possibly 80 per cent of the population would have voted for the Communist Ho Chi Minh as their leader rather than Chief of State Bao Dai."[7]

In the face of all this evidence, the Deputy Under Secretary for Political Affairs, U. Alexis Johnson, could still try to claim that "it was the North that was not willing to submit itself to the test of free elections under international control."[8]

Various writers agree, including former White House assistant Richard Goodwin, that the United States supported this stand. They use such phrases as "with American support," "with American backing," "with encouragement from the United States." Senator Gruening has said Diem's regime refused to carry out the elections "at our urging."[9] Former Ambassador George F. Kennan, testifying in the Fulbright hearings, said: "I do not think it [preventing the elections] was a wise policy.

. . . It seems to me that as people who profess to believe in the democratic process, we are in a poor position to object to the consequences of any free expression of opinion on the part of peoples elsewhere in the world."[10]

Diem could never have taken his stand without our support, obviously. Just as obviously, if we had insisted that the elections be carried out as scheduled, it could have been done. Whatever arguments have been presented since cannot hide the fact that this was one of the political decisions which led to the war we are now fighting. As Robert Scigliano, a member of the Michigan State University Vietnam Advisory Group from 1957 to 1958, has put it: "The only alternative to peaceful reunification was reunification by force."[11]

Once again, anyone who reads the evidence sees that it is not necessary to employ an articulate generalization to reveal the contradictions in the administration's case about our "commitments." These documents literally speak for themselves. I am sure that if more people would just read them, it would be better understood why we must speak out.

Another source which has been repeatedly cited as a basis of the American commitment is the SEATO Treaty. I have noted the words of Secretary Rusk, "Let us be clear about our commitment in Vietnam. It began with the Southeast Asia Treaty."

What imperatives for American action does the SEATO Treaty contain? "America keeps her word." What was the exact nature of the word given by America? Has the United States kept that word? The SEATO Treaty states in Article 1:

> The Parties undertake, as set forth in the Charter of the United Nations, to settle any international disputes in which they may be involved by peaceful means . . . and to refrain from the threat or use of force in any manner inconsistent with the purposes of the United Nations.

The relevant Articles of the U.N. Charter for the peaceful settlement of international disputes were quoted at length in the Introduction and do not need repeating here.

Article 4 of the SEATO Treaty defines the two types of threats to the treaty members and the measures which the treaty members are obligated to take in response:

> Section 1. Each party recognizes that aggression by means of armed attack in the treaty area . . . would endanger its own peace

and safety, and agrees that it will in that event act to meet the common danger in accordance with its constitutional processes. *Measures taken under this paragraph shall be immediately reported to the Security Council of the United Nations.*

Section 2. If, in the opinion of any of the parties, the inviolability or the integrity . . . of any party . . . is threatened in any way other than by armed attack . . . the *parties shall consult immediately in order to agree on the measures which should be taken for the common defense.* [Italics added.]

The unilateral resort to force by the United States without exhausting the mechanism for the peaceful settlement of disputes in the U.N. Charter is clearly a violation of the pledged word of the United States.

When the initial military actions of the United States were taken, they were not in response to threats to the peace as defined in Article 4, Section 1. Let us suppose for a moment that an *ex post facto* case of "armed aggression" can be laid to a Peking-Hanoi plot. Then the argument can be made that the response was made under Section 1. However, it is plainly stated that such measures *shall* be referred to the Security Council. This was not done.

The fighting in Vietnam is closer to the definition contained in Section 2 of Article 4. Does this "solemn word" of the United States commit us to an automatically unilateral response? The answer is an unequivocal "no." We are only asked to "consult immediately in order to agree on the measures which should be taken for the common defense."

By no possible stretch of the English language does the SEATO Treaty commit us to any unilateral action. By no possible stretch of the imagination can the SEATO Treaty be a basis for the current policy being followed in Vietnam. Senator Walter F. George, Chairman of the Foreign Relations Committee when the treaty was debated in the Senate, was very emphatic on this point when he said, "I cannot emphasize too strongly that we have no obligation . . . to take positive measures of any kind. All we are obligated to do is to consult together about it."[12]

The United States did give her word in the SEATO Treaty to act within the provisions of the U.N. Charter for the peaceful settlement of international disputes. If we ask other nations to be bound by these principles, we must keep them ourselves. Otherwise, they will become merely "scraps of paper."

The vast changes made in American policy after 1964 will be discussed at greater length in the subsequent chapters. But it is appropriate at this point to scan the acts of President Kennedy for any possible "commitment" which would justify the current American role in Vietnam.

In a letter to President Diem of December 14, 1961, President Kennedy said that:

> We are prepared to *help* the Republic of Vietnam to protect its people and to preserve its independence. We shall promptly increase our assistance to your defense effort as well as help relieve the destruction of the floods which you describe.[13] [Italics added.]

A policy to *help* the Vietnamese in their struggle is not the same as a policy which declares that the United States must defeat the enemies of South Vietnam at all costs because "it is better to do it there than it is in Honolulu."[14] In accordance with his policy of assisting the South Vietnamese, President Kennedy increased the number of American military advisors in Vietnam from about 750 in 1961 to about 17,000 by the end of 1963. It is important to remember that he did not at any time alter the role of these forces—they were solely advisors, never combat forces.

The evidence strongly points to the conclusion that President Kennedy was firmly opposed to a direct American military commitment. In November 1961, as a result of events associated with the mission of General Maxwell Taylor and Walt Rostow, the President told Professor Arthur Schlesinger:

> They want a force of American troops. They say it's necessary in order to restore confidence and maintain morale. . . . Then we will be told we have to send in more troops. It's like taking a drink. The effect wears off, and you have to take another.

Schlesinger paraphrased the rest of the President's thoughts as follows:

> The war in Vietnam, he added, could be won only so long as it was *their* war. If it were ever converted into a white man's war, we would lose as the French had lost a decade earlier.[15]

President Kennedy emphasized this position again quite strongly in a CBS interview on September 2, 1963:

> I don't think that unless a greater effort is made by the government to win popular support that the war can be won out there. In the final analysis, it is their war. They are the ones who have to win it or lose it. We can help them, we can give them equipment, we

can send our men out there as advisors, but they have to win it—the people of Vietnam—against the Communists. We are prepared to continue to assist them, but I don't think that the war can be won unless the people support the effort.[16]

The course of action that President Kennedy would have pursued if he had lived is not a fruitful question since it cannot be answered. On the other hand, we can piece together the essentials of the American conduct in Vietnam while he lived.

There is no evidence of a unilateral commitment to South Vietnam under President Kennedy. There is no evidence that the fate of South Vietnam was seen as integral to the defense of the United States or to that of the "free world."

President Kennedy was opposed to and continuously resisted the pressures to alter the status of American advisors to combat troops. In this context, it is useful to note his firmness in standing by his belief that no American troops would be committed to rescue the Cubans in case of failure at the Bay of Pigs in April 1961. He did not reverse his belief despite the fact that he was under tremendous pressure at the time to commit American fighting forces.

Finally, for a variety of reasons, he viewed the struggle as "their" war. We could not or should not win it for them. They, in turn, would not win it without massive reforms to win over the people.

In light of all this evidence, it is absolutely clear that American policy after 1964 has not been merely a continuation of commitments made before 1964. Great confusion has come about on this crucial point because there *is* an American consensus on opposition to Communism. There are many alternative policies available to oppose Communism. However, the irrefutable fact is that the current policy is a complete reversal of the pre-1964 policy.

The role of the American military in the pre-1964 policy is well summarized in an official government booklet, *Viet Nam: The Struggle For Freedom*, released in 1964. This document wisely warned against the use of American troops in a guerrilla war "in which knowledge of terrain, language, and local customs is especially important." Such an introduction of American soldiers would give "ammunition for Communist propaganda which falsely proclaims that the United States is conducting a 'white man's war' against Asians."[17]

There has been an extensive public relations campaign undertaken by the administration and others to place public support behind the current American policy in Vietnam. As a result of this effort, the conflict is often erroneously viewed by the American people as being one of American ideals and democracy versus the tyranny of Communism.

For example, Vice President Lyndon Johnson, on a visit to South Vietnam in May 1961, stated that: "Ngo Dinh Diem, who was recently reelected to office by an overwhelming majority of his countrymen despite bitter Communist opposition, is in the vanguard of those leaders who stand for freedom on the periphery of the Communist empire in Asia."[18]

Actually, Diem replaced Bao Dai as Chief of State in October 1955, in an election which saw Diem receive over 98 per cent of the vote. This "overwhelming majority" is similar to the totals run up in the "elections" in Communist countries.

We have gone over the insistence of various American leaders that the South Vietnamese should conduct thorough reforms in order to merit continuation of American economic assistance. We know that our ideals and traditions put the U.S. on the side of those who are responsive to the needs of the people. The crucial question to be answered concerns the nature of the government we have been supporting and have become identified with in Vietnam. Has this government lived up to its commitments to the welfare of the people? What are the differences between the government and those who are fighting against it? Is the Vietnamese war a struggle between the "Communist empire" and the "vanguard of freedom"?

> Here is a man [Diem] who as a statesman lives by his opposition to Communism, but who is building, down to the smallest details, a replica of the totalitarian regime which he opposes.
>
> His consolidation of power has been entirely by totalitarian means.
>
> He will have given his people little to choose between the totalitarianism of the north and his own.

These astute observations were not written in hindsight. Rather, this analysis of Diem by Professor Hans Morgenthau appeared in the *Washington Post* on February 26, 1956. For anyone who has been willing to go behind the public relations cliches, the ugly realities of the South Vietnamese government have been all too vivid. After seeing these realities, James Reston's dictum that "wrong assumptions lead to wrong decisions" becomes all the more relevant to the current policy in Vietnam.

The respected French journalist Philippe Devillers has made a judgment from his long association in Vietnam which is identical to that of Professor Morgenthau:

The fact is that the people of Vietnam have always been caught between Communism and a form of anti-Communism which they could not accept. In the days of the French, they had to choose between Communism and a hated colonialist regime; today the Americans give them a choice between Communism and a dictatorship of a type which is at one and the same time fascist and medieval.[19]

What were some of the policies and actions of Diem which made his regime just as undemocratic and repressive as that of the Communists?

Diem was a man who could brook no opposition. To him, every Vietnamese who had fought against the French was a traitor to his regime. While there were Communist members of the Viet Minh who remained in the South, Diem made the mistake of outlawing all opposition and lumping all opponents together as Vietnamese Communists. What Jean Lacouture has called a "witch hunt" began. The Can Lao, Diem's personal party, allowed no independent political parties or opposition of any kind.

The now notorious "Ordinance No. 6" was decreed by Diem on January 11, 1956. It authorized arrest or imprisonment of "any person considered to be a danger to the defense of the state or to national interests." Concentration camps were set up, and thousands of members of the opposition were sent to them for "political re-education." Local villages had traditionally chosen their own chiefs, but Diem removed them and appointed his own.

With this one stroke, Diem did more harm to the cause of democracy than any terror employed by the Communists could do. With this one stroke, Diem produced the massive resentment and alienation from the government on which Communism thrives. It is significant that these appointed officials were so unpopular that in the late 1950's their assassination by the Viet Cong was genuinely welcomed by many villagers.

Another of Diem's devices was the Public Meetings Law. This act prohibited any public gathering except with written government approval. His policies left the opposition with a choice of prison, exile, or joining the growing underground led by the Communists.

A 1957 "series of man-hunts," in theory aimed at the Communists, hit at "all those, and they were many—Democrats, Socialists, Liberals, adherents of the sects—who were bold enough to express their disagreement." In 1958 the situation grew worse, with roundups more frequent and more brutal. Their conduct, says Philippe Devillers, "very soon set the villagers against the regime."[20] Contributing to their defection was the resentment of peasants who had been given land owned by absentee landlords during the Viet Minh period of control only to have it handed back to the former owners under Diem. To be allowed under this "land reform" to purchase the acres they were already working as their own did not endear the government to them.

The cycle of events leading to civil strife was thus set in motion to a large extent by the Diem government itself. Devillers describes it succinctly in this paragraph:

> The Communists, finding themselves hunted down, began to fight back. Informers were sought out and shot in increasing numbers, and village chiefs who had presided over the denunciations, village notables, and members of the militia who took part were frequently treated in the same way. The people of the villages, thus intimidated, fell silent. Diem's police and army saw their sources of information drying up one after another. To make good the lack, they resorted to worse barbarity, hoping to inspire an even greater terror among the villagers than that inspired by the Communists. And in that fateful year of 1958 they overstepped all bounds. The peasants, disgusted to see Diem's men acting in this way, lent their assistance to the Communists and even the sects, going so far as to take up arms at their side. The opposition (and deserters) found it increasingly easier to find hideouts; they were able to set up more and more supply dumps and outposts, and even to fortify villages according to well-tried methods, transforming them into bases for their operations.[21]

Another new measure for repression was enacted on May 6, 1959, under which special military tribunals were given the task of prosecution "within three days" of persons on whom the Ministry of Defense had served charges "without preliminary inquiry." There was no appeal from the military tribunals.

It is hardly surprising, then, that the scattered guerrilla operations blossomed into civil war, or that Diem, after two earlier unsuccessful efforts—one by his own paratroopers, one a bombing attack by two of his own planes on the palace—was finally overthrown by a coup and assassinated on November 2, 1963.

No one has doubted the fact that North Vietnam was supporting the Viet Cong any more than there was a question that the United States was supporting Diem. Nor is the issue before us whether we oppose Communism in Vietnam. Rather, we must see the political realities of Vietnam, no matter how unpleasant they are. We must understand exactly what we have stood for in Vietnam.

For example, Wesley Fishel, an American academic follower of Diem, wrote in 1959 that Diem governed the "Republic in accordance with the terms of the Constitution"; Diem rejects both absolute individual and absolute state power; "he isn't operating a dictatorship"; and he was "increasing . . . the freedoms of his countrymen."[22] However, in 1964, when it was impossible to continue to hide the extent and the consequences of Diem's tyranny, this same observer admitted that Diem's rule was really "revolutionary fascism."[23]

I know that the American people do not want to be "committed" in Vietnam to this kind of tyranny and lack of interest in the welfare of the people, which is equal to that of the Communists. We must come to grips with the realities and base our policy on those realities instead of a public relations myth and illusion.

To sum up the nature of the American commitment, it was to assist a regime in Vietnam which would undertake major reforms for the good of the people. We have seen this commitment broken.

Further, the American commitment was to the peaceful settlement of international disputes and our obligations in SEATO. We have seen these commitments broken.

Again, the American commitment was to the cause of freedom and democracy in Vietnam. We have seen the real nature of the relationship between the Saigon government and the people of South Vietnam— an oppressive dictatorship under Ngo Dinh Diem.

Now let us review how the increased political failures in South Vietnam were matched by an increased application of American military force. This was the tool by which we sought to reverse the unhappy course of events—escalation.

IV

Escalation

"Escalation breeds escalation."

I reached this conclusion in a Senate speech made in February 1966.

The "road of unlimited escalation," that speech asserted, could lead to "American troop commitments rising to 400,000, 600,000, 800,000, 1 million if necessary." Should we take that road—and at the time we were already following it ever deeper into the jungles of warfare—"our chauffeur will be named military necessity and [it is a road] upon which we would travel at a faster and faster speed, throttle to the floor, and never mind the backseat jouncing, the terror and pain of either the pedestrians in the way or the backseat passengers who must take the ride willy-nilly. Nor does the road of faster and faster escalation provide necessarily more safety than comfort. There may be other traffic coming out to meet us, China for example, or even Russia. At such speed a head-on collision could be fatal not only to the driver but to us in the back seat as well."[1]

How far we have moved down the escalation road is evident. In 1961 the official record shows just one American killed and one wounded in Vietnam in the entire year; by the end of 1967 our casualties were running at an average rate of 25 dead and 172 wounded *every day*. While 5,008 died and 30,093 were wounded in 1966, the American dead for 1967 totaled 9,353—an increase of more than 85 per cent for 1967 over 1966. By then the total of American dead had reached 16,000 and the wounded just under 100,000. In February 1968 during the Viet Cong assaults on Saigon, Hué, and the provincial capitals, American deaths for one week reached a new high of 543, while the 1968 7-week total through February 17 came to 2,242.

At the end of 1961, U.S. forces in Vietnam totaled 1,364; at the end of 1966, 389,000; by January 1968 the total was 486,000, and General Westmoreland was expecting most of the 525,000 then authorized by the end of January.[2] Yet few people can tell you how we got in so deep.

It is the nature of a policy of escalation that each step up the ladder has followed from the one before, because "escalation breeds escalation" in our own policies as well as in the other side's response. Each step makes the next not only possible but more acceptable. Or, in the words of President Kennedy quoted earlier, "It's like taking a drink. The effect wears off, and you have to take another."

By the end of 1960, half of South Vietnam was under control of the guerrillas, estimated at a strength of 10,000. During the year more than 3,000 local officials met death or kidnapping at their hands. The Diem government's own figures, probably on the low side, showed some 1,600 South Vietnamese military combat deaths. During that year we took a first tentative step toward escalation.

The original Military Assistance Advisory Group sent by Truman had comprised 35 members in 1950. Ten years later it had become fairly stable at around 300, with major emphasis on training military leaders who in turn trained the Vietnamese troops. On May 5, 1960, it was announced that the MAAG, then 327 in number, would be increased to 685 by the end of the year. The figure was not plucked out of the air—this was the top number legally allowed under the Geneva Agreements. But on December 31 the U. S. forces stood at 773.

American concern was increased by the coup attempt of November 1960, in which Diem's paratroopers led a palace assault. His reply was further harsh repression of all opposition. Dr. Pham Quang Dan, the only real opposition leader in the National Assembly, was jailed, an act which Douglas Pike calls "probably the Diem government's point of no return."[3] We were already paying the bill for South Vietnam's military forces, and American contributions there equaled a quarter of the country's entire national income. "After six years of large-scale American aid," said one returning economist observer, "Vietnam is becoming a permanent mendicant. Certainly, if aid were eliminated tomorrow, there would be an unpaid army and unfed civilians."[4]

In May 1961, Vice President Lyndon B. Johnson went to Saigon on an Asian "fact finding mission." He said there that we would stand "shoulder to shoulder" with South Vietnam in its war against Communism. Jointly with Diem he announced agreement to add another $40 million, mainly to beef up the 40,000-man civil guard and 150,000-man army. But on the plane out of Saigon, when a reporter started to talk about Diem's faults, Johnson answered, "Don't tell me about Diem. He's all we've got out there."[5]

A perceptive reporter had said almost the same thing five years earlier. John Mecklin, who dealt with Diem during his last eighteen months while serving as United States Information Agency chief in Saigon, had written of this "Messiah with a persecution complex": "For lack of any alternative, we are stuck with a marginal man."[6] But because he was "all we've got out there," he continued to be presented to America—with the help of his New York public-relations firm—not as a paranoid dictatorial mandarin but as a valiant fighter against Communist encroachment from the North. Today Diem is generally omitted as far as possible in official U.S. references to that period, but in Vietnam they celebrate the anniversary of his final downfall and assassination.

In October 1961, five months after Johnson's visit, came the mission of General Taylor and Walt Rostow. "The effect [of this mission]," Professor Schlesinger has written, "was to color future thinking about Vietnam in both Saigon and Washington with the unavowed assumption that Vietnam was primarily a military rather than a political problem."[7] Another product of this mission was the development of the Rostow Plan 6 for bombing North Vietnam.

All of these actions, one by one, were drawing us closer to combat under the inevitable logic that when each step still was not enough, another would be taken. On February 4, 1962, 15 helicopters with U.S. crews—who else could operate them?—flew South Vietnamese troops in a surprise attack on Hung My. American pilots began flying "combat-training missions" involving bombing and strafing attacks. Technically, they were only observers and advisors, but in fact the less qualified Vietnamese airmen acted only as co-pilots. Our helicopters usually carried American crewmen to man machine guns for returning groundfire, according to a March 6 *Wall Street Journal* report. Also in March came a report of American "advisors" parachuting into combat with 500 South Vietnamese troops near the Cambodian frontier. From there, with this emphasis on a military solution and a disregard for political reforms, our Vietnamese intervention could go only one way: up. From 1,364 under MAAG at the beginning of 1962, the number of American military swelled under MACV to 9,865 at year's end.[8]

Our helicopter fleet had grown with the addition of the first "Hueys," the turbine-powered HU-IAs, each carrying 16 rockets as well as heavy machine guns. They bore no U.S. insignia but were flown by U.S. crews. In 1962, a later State Department report revealed: "U.S. Army aviation units flew over 50,000 sorties in support of operations in Vietnam, approximately half of which were combat support sorties."[9] In March 1963, 100 25th Infantry Division men came in to serve specifically as machine gunners aboard Army helicopters ferrying Vietnamese troops into fighting areas, thus freeing mechanics who had doubled as gunners. Marine air units had also joined the operation. In answer to our appeal for "a helping hand," 30 Australian guerrilla-warfare specialists had arrived in Saigon in August to help train South Vietnamese troops.

There are two fundamental flaws in a policy of escalation. The reliance on the use of military force means that the more basic political reforms are pushed deeper into the background. Secondly, there is nothing which prevents the other side from responding to our escalation with their own escalation.

Figures show the escalation was not one-sided. In early 1961 Viet Cong strength was estimated at 9,000; by May it was 12,000, according to Secretary Rusk; 13,000–15,000 in August, by a *New York Times* report; in August 1962 the same paper gave a figure of 20,000. Senator Mansfield's report of his late 1962 visit with other Senators to Vietnam put the Viet Cong strength at "22,000 to 24,000 regulars with a supplement of local irregulars of over 100,000."[10] Six months later, on June 16, 1964, Secretary McNamara put the Viet Cong force at 65,000 regulars and 80,000–100,000 part-time guerrillas. Senator Mansfield's report on his 1965 year-end Vietnam mission estimated the regulars at 73,000 out of a total 230,000. Of these, only 14,000 were believed to be from the North Vietnamese army.[11] In November 1966, a Saigon dispatch called the total 270,000, including 45,000 reportedly Northern army personnel. "Escalation breeds escalation."

As Senator Mansfield's 1966 report put it: "Total Vietcong strength, apparently, is steadily increasing despite the serious casualties which these forces have suffered during the past few months."

Why has the United States followed a course of escalation? What is the rationale behind this policy? What did we hope to gain from military escalation?

One of the most succinct and authoritative statements on the administration's theory of escalation was made in the speech to Congress of General William Westmoreland on April 28, 1967. The General said that "the rate of decline [of the morale and the military structure of the enemy] will be in proportion to the pressure directed against him."

This theory is an absolute contradiction to the actual history of the Vietnam conflict. A *New York Times* editorial on April 29, 1967 correctly pointed out this weakness in the General's assertion: "He calls for a steady step-up of pressure on North Vietnam as the surest road to 'defeat' of the Communist forces. Yet he acknowledges that overall enemy strength in South Vietnam has doubled during the two years that the United States has been bombing the North and building up its combat forces in the South to 438,000."

In 1961 there were less than 10,000 Viet Cong guerrillas. The absence of political reforms by the succession of Saigon regimes, the alienation from the government that is not really a government, the indifference of the populace, produced a condition of which the 1966 Mansfield report said that "a total collapse of the Saigon government's authority appeared imminent in the early months of 1965." The American response was to change the role of American advisors to combat troops and to escalate the number of soldiers in Vietnam. One of the measures of the effectiveness of this policy was the fact that the less than 10,000 guerrillas of 1961 had grown to a force near 300,000 in the summer of 1967.

Thus instead of causing a decline in the power of the enemy, the policy of escalation has brought about an increase in the enemy forces. Clearly the theory of military escalation is founded on a dangerous illusion. Others have constantly called our attention to the strong contrast between the theory of escalation and its results.

As a *New York Times* editorial on December 3, 1965 stated, "Escalation has not been the road to peace nor to surrender by North Vietnam. Exactly the opposite has happened." On June 30, 1966 the *Times* again warned that "Each step in American escalation of the war has failed of its purpose." Again on March 8, 1967 the *Times* observed that "The world knows that the United States cannot lose in the sense of being forced to surrender or withdraw from Vietnam, but does anyone really know that the Vietcong and Hanoi can lose? Thus far, the harder the blows the more stubborn the resistance."

Instead of defeating the enemy, a policy of military escalation, as Arthur Schlesinger says, means that "our method defeats our goal." He rejects "the theory that widening the war will shorten it." In calling for de-escalation, he comments that there have been reports "that Vietcong morale is declining as long as I can remember." "Each step," he says, "was reasonably regarded at the time as being the last that would be necessary; yet, in retrospect, each step led only to the next, until we find ourselves entrapped today in that nightmare of American strategists, a land war in Asia."[12]

"The value of victory," says Herman Kahn in his book *On Escalation*, "is usually great enough so that it would be worth while for either side to raise its commitment enough to win the escalation *if it were certain that the other side would not counter the rise*"[13]—emphasizing the last phrase with italics. But that "if" is the trouble. Rather than assuming the other side will not counter the rise, there is a well-demonstrated certainty that it will.

After 1962 there are three points at which highly significant U.S. escalation took place.[14] One was August 4, 1964, when for the first time, in retaliation for attacks on two American destroyers in the Gulf of Tonkin, we hit North Vietnamese territory. The second was the carrier-based bombing raid of February 7, 1965 against North Vietnam's Dong Hoi base, from which the beginning daily bombing of North Vietnam was to grow routine. The third was the authorized commitment of our ground troops to direct combat action, the sanction of which by President Johnson was reported on June 8, 1965.

The Tonkin Bay "incident" has special importance because it led to the Congressional resolution on which President Johnson since has relied so heavily as the authorization for all of our subsequent initiative in bombing and combat operations. That resolution "approves and supports the determination of the President, as Commander in Chief, to take all necessary measures to repel any armed attack against the forces of the United States and to prevent further aggression." Senator Morse called it "naught but a resolution which embodies a predated declaration of war," and it has in effect been so treated by the President. Senators Morse and Gruening cast the only two dissenting votes in the entire Congress. If it were presented again today, I am sure they would be joined by many more dissenters.

Actually, so far as the Tonkin Bay situation was concerned, the President had already acted, and to most of us the resolution appeared more as approving the August 4 raids after the fact than as conferring unlimited escalation power in the future. It was support for the President in the midst of news headlines, and its denial by Congress then would have been counter to popular emotion. Whether so designed or not, the resolution has been repeatedly used to bolster new acts of escalation as well as justifying the one that had just occurred.

On January 27, 1964 Secretary McNamara had told a House committee that the U.S., after training Vietnamese with increased vigor since 1961, hoped to be able to withdraw most of its troops by the end of 1965. He did not believe, he said, that we "should assume the primary responsibility for the war in South Vietnam." But the political instability in the wake of Diem's fall found us, instead, propping up in turn, with greater and greater effort, five new regimes in the space of 17 months. Only three days after McNamara's testimony General Nguyen Khanh, with 3,000 of his troops, seized the government from Premier Tho, Diem's successor. But by July there were well-founded rumors that it would soon be Khanh's turn to go next.

Khanh's need for broadened Vietnamese support was great. On July 19, speaking to 100,000 at a Saigon rally marking the tenth anniversary of the Geneva Accords, he called for attack on the North. A million refugees in the South, he said, held "the dream of liberating their native land." Air Commodore Nguyen Cao Ky, who ended the rapid overturn of governments a year later for a longer stay in power, said that his planes were ready to bomb North Vietnam. Ambassador Taylor protested such war talk as contrary to U.S. policy, but Khanh was reported as saying that the only conflict was on timing and on what to announce publicly. Had we already decided on escalation to the North? Were we just waiting for, or about to manufacture, a good pretext?

On July 30 South Vietnamese naval vessels did take the war north by bombing two islands, Hon Me and Hon Ngu, situated 3 and 5 miles off the North Vietnamese coast. In the later Senate debate, following secret hearings which he attended, Senator Wayne Morse declared "categorically that high officials of this Government have admitted on the record that they were aware of plans for the bombardment."[15]

The destroyer *Maddox* had on occasions patrolled inside the 12-mile limit claimed by North Vietnam (in common with some other countries) to demonstrate our own claim to a 3-mile limit, despite the provocative effect of this action. It has not been made clear just where the *Maddox* was during the shelling, except that she was "in international waters"— possibly by our definition, not that of the North Vietnamese. Our presence nearby "was bound to implicate us," as Senator Morse put it. The *Maddox* set out for open waters as a result of "intelligence that we were getting." Was it that North Vietnam's naval vessels were starting out to drive us from what they consider their coastal waters? "Finally, on Sunday, the PT boats [of North Vietnam] were close enough for the first engagement to take place," Senator Morse told the Senate. The three

PT boats fired shells and torpedoes which did no damage to the *Maddox;* but one of them was sunk, the others damaged.

This "unprovoked" attack was a mystery to many editorial writers who could not understand the Communist foolhardiness in taking on the United States Navy. A Pentagon spokesman next day called the incident "unwelcome, but not especially serious." Premier Khanh wanted more action. "The Americans," he said publicly, "should seize this occasion to dissipate the enemy's belief according to which the United States is only a paper tiger."[16] North Vietnam, admitting the attack, declared that it took place in North Vietnamese waters.

Two days later the Defense Department announced a second naval raid on the *Maddox* and a sister destroyer, the *C. Turner Joy.* Again, there was no damage to the U.S. ships—for the two raids the only damage was one shell lodged in the hull of one of our vessels—and two PT boats were reported sunk. This time retribution was swift, as we showed we were indeed, if proof were needed, no "paper tiger." A 5-hour raid over a 100-mile stretch of North Vietnam by 64 sorties from Seventh Fleet carriers hit four of Hanoi's naval bases, destroyed or damaged half its navy (25 PT boats), and all but wiped out an oil storage depot with about 10 per cent of the country's oil storage facilities.

As the planes were an hour on their way to target, Lyndon B. Johnson, newly nominated for election to the Presidency he had inherited, took over the television networks to report dramatically that "as I speak to you tonight" air action was taking place, even though "we seek no wider war." "And just a few minutes ago I was able to reach Senator Goldwater and I am glad to say that he has expressed his support of the statement I am making to you tonight."[17]

The atmosphere of the nation reminded columnist Marquis Childs of the "moment of patriotic fervor" as the Korean war began. The *Vienna Volksblatt* commented: "If Johnson rattles his saber a little it is mainly to show the electorate that he is not the defeatist and friend of Communists that Goldwater has made him out to be." From Saigon, Seymour Topping of *The New York Times* wrote that "General Khanh has been given a political lift by the attack made by North Vietnamese PT boats."[18] And the *Christian Science Monitor* prophesied: "The United States is unavoidably going in further. The only questions are when and how far."

This was escalation to the North, and it was also reprisal, a reprisal in which, after sinking enemy ships while taking one shell harmlessly—something of a reprisal in itself—we destroyed half Hanoi's navy and a tenth of her oil storage. Reprisals, according to the *Rules of Land Warfare* which is quoted by the State Department authoritatively, should never be taken "merely for revenge" and "should not be excessive or exceed the degree of violence committed by the enemy." These were principles which we applied at the Nuremberg trials.[19]

The United Nations has repeatedly condemned reprisals, in which the attacking nation becomes sole judge and jury, similar to an "Old West" lynching party, rather than supporting the orderly processes of international law for which the U.N. is structured. When reprisals have been the outlaw acts of other nations, the United States has joined in their condemnation. But in Vietnam consistently from the start we have acted in complete disregard of the principles we profess, continually eroding the United Nations' peacekeeping function as no other nation or postwar conflict has done to such detriment.

Our inconsistency, our "arrogance of power" when our cause will not stand U.N. scrutiny, is underlined by a Security Council resolution which we had supported only four months earlier, in April 1964. Britain, after Yemeni attacks over the border into its protectorate of Aden, had attacked a fort at Harib in Yemen in reprisal. Ambassador Adlai Stevenson told the Security Council the United States had "repeatedly expressed" its emphatic disapproval of "retaliatory raids, wherever they occur and by whomever they are committed." Then we voted for the resolution which condemned "reprisals as incompatible with the purposes and principles of the United Nations."

More recently, on November 25, 1966, we voted to censure Israel for her reprisal raid on Samu, Jordan. There, we put our approval on a resolution "reaffirming the previous resolutions of the Security Council condemning past incidents of reprisal in breach of . . . the United Nations Charter." Our Tonkin Bay action certainly paralleled the Jordan incident, which "constituted a large-scale and carefully planned military action."[20] But when the Tonkin Bay case was debated in the Security Council on August 7, 1964, we did not hold to our professed principles. Only Britain and Nationalist China supported us.

The February 7, 1965 start of the now commonplace bombing of North Vietnam came after new political turmoil in South Vietnam. The events of January had included a series of antigovernment and anti-American "pro-neutralist" demonstrations; a general strike in Hué and Danang, where Vietnamese employees quit work at our air base; leaflets attacking the civilian Huong regime as "servile collaborators with the Americans"; stoning of the USIA library in Saigon; and invasion of the

U.S. consulate during a demonstration of 5,000 in Hué, resulting in windows and furniture broken and setting fire to the 6,000-book library on the first floor. General Khanh, out of power, said "something must be done" or else the "upsurge of anti-Americanism" "will slow down our war against the Communists." The Huong government fell to a military group on January 27. Both the government and our own situation were obviously shaky again. After the Viet Cong raid on our base at Pleiku and our retaliatory carrier-based strike on Dong Hoi, Presidential aide McGeorge Bundy, who had arrived in Saigon shortly before these events, said on his return two days after them "that the immediate effect of the Pleiku and North Vietnamese raids was to pull together American and Vietnamese leaders."[21]

The North Vietnam bombings of February 7 and 8 were justified by U.S. leaders as retaliation for the Pleiku night attack in which a barracks was blown up, killing 8 Americans and wounding 126, while nine helicopters and a transport plane were destroyed and others damaged. But there were some who raised doubts. Could the bombing have been planned in advance, and ordered at the first convenient opportunity when "justification" could be given? Were we possibly just waiting for a chance to "retaliate"? Charles Roberts, a White House reporter for eleven years, has said that "the President . . . told me in May, 1965, that he had made the decision to bomb four months before Pleiku . . . in October, 1964, at the height of the Presidential election campaign."[22]

The attack was by a force estimated at 100 or fewer Viet Cong. There had been other far larger night guerrilla raids in the past, in which whole South Vietnamese units up to company size were wiped out.

The heaviest weapons used were captured U.S. 81-mm. mortars. "Would this," asked *The New York Times'* Charles Mohr, a Vietnam journalistic veteran, "sustain the argument that North Vietnam made possible this particular attack?"[23]

There were questions raised concerning our own lax security. Some of the guerrillas had crawled right on to the base to place explosive charges against barracks walls and on the airstrip.

The attack news reached Washington late Saturday afternoon, which was early Sunday in Vietnam. "Clearly, American planes must already have been poised for the attack, since no more than twelve hours elapsed between the *beginning* of the mortar shelling of Pleiku and the first dropping of bombs."[24]

The planes came from Seventh Fleet carriers, all three of which just happened to be in the South China Sea near the Vietnamese coast. "The usual pattern," wrote Mohr, "is one of dispersal, with each carrier forming the nucleus of an attack force operating off different parts of east Asia."

Whatever weight is given by history to our real or ostensible motivations, it is certain that most Americans cannot view equably the naked use of U.S. military power, particularly against a small country. To be acceptable, such use must be clothed in rationalizations proving that we are reluctantly forced into the aggressive actions we deplore in others. Further, we must be convinced that our ultimate purposes are benevolent: the damage we inflict must be made to look pale beside the specter of the damage which will occur if we do not act. In Vietnam, because the Communism of the North is unconscionably evil, we must somehow defeat it since the South Vietnamese could never do it without us.

I do not question the President's sincerity, and I join him when he says "we want no wider war." But there can be no doubt that we have initiated major escalation on several occasions, and continued it, resulting in precisely the "wider war" we do not want. We have done it in the mistaken notion that escalation of military effort will attain the objective of obliterating Communism in Vietnam. All the evidence lies to the contrary.

For escalation is, as psychologist Charles E. Osgood has put it, "a baited hook." "The hook is psychological: The effects of escalation are such as to produce the very conditions, both internally and externally, which make it harder and harder to stop moving upward. Internally, particularly in a democracy, escalation produces aggressive emotions in the populace (exacerbated by deaths of loved ones) which make retreat political suicide. Externally, escalation produces hardening, rather than softening, in the opponent's resolve and willingness to take risks—which are likely to carry us far beyond the level originally intended."[25]

Those effects are fully evident in 1968. The commonest phrase in my Vietnam mail from the "hawks" is "When are we going to win the war, and why not?"—a sentence which manages to combine "aggressive emotion" with recognition that after all the task of "winning" may well be foredoomed to failure. At the same time, the hardening of purpose by Hanoi is attested by all responsible reporters who have visited the North.

A moderate French deputy, Jacques Duhamel, returning from a Hanoi visit in late November 1966, reported in *Le Figaro* that U.S. air and naval attacks are "more than a moral fault, [they are] a political error, since they are hardening the determination of the people more than they are weakening its economy. . . ." Industrial and military aid from Russia and consumer goods from China are apparently increasing.[26]

"Escalation breeds escalation." The baited hook is always dangling attractively within reach. It is human nature to continue following past practice, and the tendency, once escalation is adopted, is to stick with it. "Psychologically, we can become glued to the escalator."[27]

Communism is a detestable denial of freedom to men, but in a democracy we must make every effort to see ourselves in the cold perspective of truth, "warts and all," lest we lose the virtues and the freedoms we extol. I share the "quiet worry" of Neil Sheehan about what we are doing to *ourselves* by this war and its escalation. In World War II and Korea, when aggression was an established fact, we could fight with a clear conscience for human freedom and dignity. But when our moral superiority is replaced by the amorality of great-power politics, when the Vietnamese, North and South alike, become pawns in the struggle for supremacy between nuclear powers, then we need to examine the problem profoundly.

Otherwise we will find ourselves in the position described by Mark Twain, and not at all in jest, when he wrote in *The Mysterious Stranger* of the "grotesque self-deception" by which the fevers of war distort the consciences of those who wage it.

V

The Credibility Gap

The scene, as described by television newsman Morley Safer, was the home of Barry Zorthian, minister-counselor of the U.S. Embassy in Saigon, the man who has been called by *Time* "the information czar" in Vietnam, on a "sticky July evening" in 1964. Gathered there were a number of newsmen invited by Mr. Zorthian for a "bull session" with the top Pentagon information officer, Assistant Secretary of Defense for Public Affairs Arthur D. Sylvester.

There had been a running clash between the efforts of the news media to give the whole, unvarnished truth and the efforts of officials to have reported only what they felt would help promote backing for official policies. Peter Kalischer of CBS put it in a phrase when he said, "The brass wants you to get on the team." In the background were such incidents as our first B-52 raids, in which, Safer's account relates, "Pentagon releases were in direct contradiction to what had happened on the ground in Vietnam." The session in Saigon was intended to help clarify the problems of press-Pentagon conflict.

Sylvester

... went on to the effect that American correspondents had a patriotic duty to disseminate only information that made the United States look good.

A network television correspondent said, "Surely, Arthur, you don't expect the American press to be the handmaidens of government."

"That's exactly what I expect," came the reply.

An agency man raised the problem that had preoccupied Ambassador Taylor and Barry Zorthian—about the credibility of American officials. Responded the Assistant Secretary of Defense for Public Affairs:

"Look, if you think any American official is going to tell you the truth, then you're stupid. Did you hear that?—stupid."[1]

This was not the first time the Pentagon's chief information officer had expressed such a view. On December 6, 1962 Mr. Sylvester spoke to a dinner meeting of the journalism fraternity Sigma Delta Chi in New York. There he said, "It's the inherent right of the Government to lie to save itself."[2] He expressed similar sentiments on other occasions.[3]

As U Thant has publicly reminded us, the first casualty of war is truth. The sophisticated observer has long since developed a well-justified skepticism of official handouts.

The credibility gap might be defined as the difference between official statements and the degree to which they are believed. For many readers, the presumption of truth lies with whatever appears in print, and its sanctity is reinforced when the printed word is official. If credibility crumbles, the very authority of government is irreparably damaged. The tendency to believe continues to sustain us even while among the more discerning the credibility gap becomes greater with each new revelation of candor's lack.

Distortions need not be lies, and most of the time they are not. Rather, we are given only the most favorable facts, half-truths rather than the whole picture. When mention of the unfavorable is unavoidable, it is downgraded as far as possible. Or we are led by technically true wording to deliberately false understanding. The attitude here is akin to the explanation of a proud but mediocre chess player who lost three games in a row: "Well, I didn't win the first game, and my opponent didn't lose the second. As to the third game, I asked him to agree to a draw, but he wouldn't."

Because of the attitude of the administration that has produced the credibility gap, one of the most complicated and difficult areas to comprehend is the negotiating positions of the two sides. Unfortunately, each side says that the failure to reach a negotiated settlement lies entirely with the other side; also, both sides often place appeals to world public opinion before quiet and sincere diplomacy.

Yet, if it is an arduous task to sort out the realities from these ambiguities, it is a task which must be done. A genuine solution can be achieved only by working from these realities. If we can discover neglected opportunities for a settlement from a comprehension of these realities, then we must use these facts to convince the administration to pursue more diligently the opportunities that are available.

Obviously no one outside of the government can expect to know the exact nature of the negotiating position of the administration. But there is a substantial amount of evidence to assist us in understanding this position.

Take the case of Secretary General U Thant's peace efforts in the fall of 1964, which became known only with the publication of Eric Sevareid's disclosure of the story more than a year later, as it had been told to him by Adlai Stevenson in London two days before his death.[4] Out of his deep concern and on his own initiative, U Thant secured agreement from North Vietnam to send an emissary to talk with an American counterpart in Rangoon about how the war might be ended. Washington wanted to wait until after the Presidential election. Then Hanoi was still willing, but the word from our side was that we would have to tell Saigon, whose shaky government would be demoralized as a result. So instead of seizing the opportunity, we went on to bolster morale in Saigon by the bombing attacks on North Vietnam.

Looking back, it appears now that Secretary General U Thant had this abortive effort in mind when he told a press conference less than three weeks after the February 7, 1965 bombing that he had presented "concrete ideas and proposals to some of the principal parties directly involved in the question of Vietnam," including the United States. Then came a veiled reference to his disappointment, one in which the credibility gap shows through: "I am sure that the great American people, if they only knew the true facts and the background to the developments in South Vietnam [i.e., the bombing], will agree with me that further bloodshed is unnecessary."[5]

The official explanation for the failure to meet with the representatives of the D.R.V. was that Secretary Rusk's "sensitive antennae" had received "no meaningful proposals."

Murrey Marder, diplomatic correspondent for the *Washington Post*, later wrote of this White House phrasing, "no meaningful proposals": "To the diplomatically initiated, that was a dead giveaway. The administration was trying to knock the story down, without flatly denying it, by making it appear that it was denying it."[6]

There can be little doubt that the North Vietnamese terms at the meeting would have been a political settlement in line with the actual power of the Saigon regime and the National Liberation Front. Consequently the United States did not participate in the Rangoon conference, just as it had supported Diem's refusal in 1955 to consult on the scheduled election for unification, because the result would have been Communist predominance in any new government.

The only alternative to a recognition of the Communist predominance was to substitute American combat troops to reverse the failures of a bankrupt Saigon government. This is the course which the administration followed instead of working for a negotiated settlement.

There are two principal lessons from this incident. The stronger power, on this occasion the N.L.F., will not offer concessions but will demand fulfillment of its ultimate aims. Secondly, contrary to the continuous assertions by administration leaders, there have been movements toward peace (even if on their own terms) by the other side.

This second point is very important because there must be at least a minimum of trust for two parties engaged in a war to be able to negotiate. In light of the outcome of efforts like that of Secretary General Thant and the history of Western failures to keep pledges to the D. R. V. discussed earlier, I believe Presidential advisor Walt Rostow is completely mistaken when he says, "I don't think that there is the slightest doubt in Hanoi, Peiping, Moscow, or any other relevant place in the world, that our President is serious and is prepared to take any steps [to negotiate]." As James Reston has accurately noted, one of the fundamental reasons for North Vietnamese reticence regarding negotiations is that they have been twice deceived in negotiations with the West, both in 1946 and 1954.

Another crucial opportunity for negotiations was the 37-day bombing pause in our attacks on the North which began December 24, 1965, during which we mounted a dramatic and highly publicized "peace offensive." In the greatest of urgency and publicity, U.S. emissaries personally representing President Johnson flew off in all directions to consult in foreign capitals. Ambassador Goldberg conferred with Pope Paul, Premier Aldo Moro of Italy, and President Charles de Gaulle in Paris. Ambassador-at-Large W. Averell Harriman flew to Warsaw, to Yugoslavia, and on to several Asian and Southeast Asian capitals. Presidential Assistant McGeorge Bundy conferred with Canadian Prime Minister Lester Pearson in Ottawa. Vice President Humphrey went west to Japan, Nationalist China, South Korea, and the Philippines. It was a breathtaking display, this high-level one-week peace blitz.

It was asserted that we were diligently searching for any reaction on which we could build toward a permanent settlement with Hanoi. "The sort of sign the United States is looking for" was said to be "either an oral proposal of negotiations . . . or some tangible sign of a decrease in military activity *or infiltration from the north.*"[7]

Secretary of State Dean Rusk explained on January 31, 1966 that the bombing was resumed because "the response has been negative, harsh, unyielding . . . They [Hanoi and the N.L.F] made clear their negative view by deeds as well as words throughout the period of suspension of bombing. Infiltrations of men and material from the North into South Viet Nam continued at a high level."[8]

Nearly a year later, in its December 5, 1966 issue, *Newsweek* reported: "According to troop infiltration figures *kept secret until now* [my italics], during last Christmas's 37-day bombing pause only some 500 enemy soldiers infiltrated from North Vietnam—although the monthly average had been 1,500."[9] Was this "infiltration . . . at a high level"? Or was it the kind of sign we said we were seeking and denied we received?

In February the infiltration figure shot up to 8,000, sixteen times that of the entire 37 previous days, when it had dropped by two thirds. It would be interesting to know whether the 500 entered South Vietnam largely in the first days of the pause, emptying the infiltration pipeline, and then tapered off.

We did not stop bombing in the South. We did not halt our own introduction of troops. In fact, while North Vietnam was "infiltrating" 500 men we were openly landing more than 14,000—equivalent to all the North Vietnamese then in the country from all previous infiltration.

This reduction in infiltration was obviously not a sign of North Vietnamese moderation, reasonableness or willingness to compromise. Perhaps the reduction was accompanied by an unyielding position or even a refusal to negotiate. It is impossible to know the exact nature of the North Vietnamese position. As I have said, these issues are tremendously complicated.

Nevertheless, we can be certain of one fact: the North Vietnamese did make some movement toward peace (reduction in infiltration), just as the United States did make some movement toward peace (the bombing pause). However, the bombing was resumed on January 31, and the opportunity to discover the position of the other side in face-to-face discussions was lost.

In other words, there have been gestures expressing a willingness for peace on both sides, even if these gestures concealed demands for surrender rather than for negotiations. The important point is that the other side has at least made a gesture. This is not the same as Secretary Rusk's assertion that of "28 proposals" for a step toward peace, "to all of these we have said yes and Hanoi has said no."[10]

A third development affording significant insight into the administration's negotiating position arose from the six-day bombing pause during the New Year's Truce in February 1967. At that time, President Johnson sent a direct letter to President Ho Chi Minh. Before this communication was answered, the bombing of the North was resumed. One month later, on March 21, the D.R.V. released the text of the Johnson letter and Ho's reply.[11]

Before examining this revealing correspondence, we should recall the public terms put forward earlier by the United States for a cessation of the bombing.

In a major speech before the U.N. General Assembly on September 22, 1966 Ambassador Goldberg stated:

> We are prepared to order a cessation of all bombing of North Vietnam—the moment we are assured, privately or otherwise, that this step will be answered promptly by a corresponding and appropriate de-escalation on the other side.[12]

This offer has two parts. We will stop the bombing first simply on the basis of a verbal assurance. Second, the *quid pro quo* is not the end of infiltration but merely de-escalation.

On February 2, 1967 President Johnson said that "just almost any step" by the other side would bring about a cessation of the bombing. In an interview published on February 8, 1967 Foreign Minister Nguyen Duy Trinh of the D.R.V. said that if the bombing ceased, "favorable conditions" would be created for negotiations. Trinh declared that "President Johnson said he was only awaiting a sign. Well, he's had the sign. We've shown our goodwill. The United States must do the same."[13]

In mid-February 1967, following release of the Trinh interview, former *Life* correspondent Lee Lockwood was in Hanoi. Lockwood wrote of the reply of a North Vietnamese official when asked what gesture toward peace the D.R.V. was willing to make:

> For the first and only time, Colonel Lao seemed incredulous and angry. "But we have *made* our offer!" he said, emphasizing every word. "We have taken a very big step! We can go no further! Why don't you people understand this?"[14]

With this background in mind, let us examine the exact nature of the terms contained in the letter of President Johnson to Ho Chi Minh.

> In the past two weeks, I have noted public statements by representatives of your Government suggesting that you would be prepared to enter direct bilateral talks with representatives of the U.S. Government, provided that we ceased "unconditionally" and

permanently our bombing operations against your country and all military actions against it. In the last day, serious and responsible parties have assured us indirectly that this is in fact your proposal.

I am prepared to order a cessation of bombing against your country and the stopping of further augmentation of United States forces in South Vietnam as soon as I am assured that infiltration into South Vietnam by land and by sea has stopped.[15]

The two parts of this offer by the President are in direct contrast to the previously stated position: the bombing was to be stopped after instead of before actions were taken by the D.R.V.; the new *quid pro quo* was not de-escalation but the end of all infiltration and supply to the forces in South Vietnam by the other side. This offer is therefore a clear demand that North Vietnam must give up the struggle in the South *before* negotiations.

From the first paragraph of the President's letter quoted above, from the statement of Foreign Minister Trinh, and from other sources, it is impossible to deny that the D.R.V. was willing to take certain acts of de-escalation based upon *previous* American utterances and then to enter into direct negotiations regarding an end to the war. This does not mean that the D.R.V. and the N.L.F. were ready to seek mutual compromises or that a negotiated settlement would have been produced from these gestures. However, the demands in the President's letter for North Vietnamese surrender and the resumption of bombing before Ho Chi Minh replied meant that any opportunity to enter into negotiations was destroyed by the intransigence of the administration.

In essence, the President demanded not reciprocity, not meaningful negotiations, but complete surrender by the other side. In calling for an end to infiltration, the President prohibited the North Vietnamese from supplying the forces in the South while there was no agreement that the United States would end all supply operations. The Viet Cong would be left without supplies, while there was no assurance in the Johnson offer that they would not be crushed in offensive operations. The terms of the President's letter, like those of the D.R.V. on previous occasions, were an attempt to gain at the conference table what had not been won in the stalemated war.

On December 11, 1966 *The New York Times* commented editorially that "a negotiated settlement means compromise." This seems a fair, reasonable definition of the word negotiation. What do these incidents reveal about the nature of the American negotiating position? Does the administration desire a negotiated (compromise) settlement? Has the administration pursued every opportunity for a negotiated (compromise) settlement? Is the only obstacle to a negotiated (compromise) settlement the attitude of the other side?

On April 4, 1965 McGeorge Bundy, then Special Assistant to the President for National Security Affairs, was asked, "If North Vietnam leaves its neighbors alone as we demand, before negotiations, what will we negotiate on?" Bundy's candid reply was that we would negotiate on "what the diplomats call the modalities. How do you make sure that there has been a stop to some of the things that are a part of this aggression, to the infiltration of troops and supplies. . . . How do you make progress toward a durable pacification of the countryside? How do you work out international ways and means of possible assurance against a renewal of this kind of threat to the peace? These are difficult and important and demanding tasks."[16]

This honest and straightforward answer lays bare the meaning of negotiations to the administration. I do not believe that the public is aware of this fact because we are subjected to a barrage of generalizations—that we are for negotiations but that the problem is with the "other side," or that there is no one to negotiate with. Bundy's frank answer is not a plea for reciprocity, mutual concessions, compromise, or negotiations. The modalities become the terms, even though they are only the "ways and means" of carrying out the prior surrender by the D.R.V. and the N.L.F. of all their interests. By no possible interpretation can this be construed as a meaningful negotiation of conflicting positions.

With this realization of the intransigence of the administration, paralleled by the previous (and untested) intransigence of the other side, Bundy accurately concluded in an article in *Foreign Affairs* in January 1967 that it is "unlikely that they will negotiate until their or our purpose has changed." As Secretary Rusk has said so often, a peace settlement will come after the North Vietnamese "abandon their attempt to take over South Vietnam by force."[17] In other words, they must first surrender all of their interests, including the Geneva pledge for unification. During his farewell interview, Ambassador Henry Cabot Lodge said that if the N.L.F. ever participated in the government of South Vietnam, "it would mean total defeat."[18]

This evidence leads one to the unfortunate conclusion that the policy of the administration is not for meaningful negotiations but for total surrender by the other side to the Saigon regime. Instead of these facts being clearly understood, the general public is confused because of the repetition of the cliches by the administration about the intransigence of the other side. Like a never changing recording, the American people are told that the only obstacle to peace lies with the "other side."

I have always held that in the formulation of national policy our primary question must be, "Is this in the national interest?" Looking at the mounting casualty lists, at the continuing ability of the Viet Cong to penetrate the security of South Vietnam's cities, at the recent appearance of Chinese-made rockets with a range of several miles, at our hard-put 5,000 Marines surrounded at Khe Sanh (as this is written) by 40,000 North Vietnamese troops—in the light of such facts, the question is whether even further escalation is truly in the national interest, or whether it is better served by making those compromises which are essential to negotiation. Is it truly in the interest of the United States to escalate actions ever closer to a World War III in order to preserve the Saigon regime?

I cannot conceive that after a careful and thorough consideration we would choose to adopt that course which threatens to lead to the outbreak of World War III. A decision of this over-riding importance and seriousness should be debated and settled according to the procedures of the Constitution. If the formal decision were made, following Constitutional procedures, to issue a declaration of war against the D.R.V. and her allies Russia and China, I would naturally support my country. But until that gruesome day, I shall do all in my power to work for the end of the self-defeating policy of military escalation by the administration. This policy and the attendant drift of events can also lead to the *very same* result as a formal declaration of war—the outbreak of World War III.

The three examples I have presented undeniably prove that there have been movements toward a negotiated settlement by the other side despite official statements. The opportunity to test the position of the other side, to see if there can be a peaceful settlement of the war, has been lost because of the intransigence of the administration. These incidents, and others as well, reveal that instead of seeking meaningful negotiations, the administration has demanded the surrender of the aims of the other side before negotiations. Negotiations as envisioned by the administration would not involve compromise on substantive issues but would merely deal with arrangements on the "modalities," the terms of surrender by the D.R.V. and the N.L.F.

What are the consequences of the avoidance of meaningful negotiations and a policy demanding unconditional surrender?

First, as Bundy has correctly observed, there will be no negotiations until one side or the other gives up its purposes. Thus far, the amount of force being used by the United States has not been enough to defeat the Viet Cong—to force them to abandon their purposes. Since there has been a rejection of the alternative of meaningful negotiations, the only alternative available to achieve the aims of the administration is more military escalation.

The inherent dilemma of a policy of escalation—that escalation is available as the response to escalation—has been discussed above. The course of the war in Vietnam has proved the validity of the late Bernard Fall's maxim that "primitiveness carries its own kind of invulnerability." The massive application of force against the Viet Cong and North Vietnam has not penetrated this invulnerability, has not convinced them to give up their aims. Therefore, future escalation must move inexorably in the direction of destroying the principal assets which the enemy has—the people and society of North Vietnam. There are few who would disagree that such a dangerous action would produce events leading to World War III.

If only the public could understand that the administration is not pursuing a policy of meaningful negotiations, then the national debate could focus much more productively on two important questions. First, should the United States have a policy that seeks meaningful negotiations? Or, in the words of President Kennedy, should we examine our own attitude in the search for peace? Second, if we really do not want meaningful negotiations, is it really in the vital interest of the United States to take actions that will probably initiate World War III in order to preserve a Saigon regime from its N.L.F. adversaries?

That desire for all-out victory, for a rejection of meaningful negotiations, and for an invitation to begin World War III is inextricably bound to the theory that we are resisting a war of aggression and the opening blow for world conquest. As we have been told, it is better to fight the Viet Cong in South Vietnam "than it is in Honolulu."

Earlier we examined the historical roots of this struggle. Now let us examine the exact nature of this war in light of the charge of aggression. Do the circumstances of this war demand that the United States maintain a policy of military escalation at the probable cost of eventually provoking World War III?

VI

Guerrilla Warfare in the South

Escalation in Vietnam—bombing the North and the Americanization of the war in the South with the commitment of over one-half
million American soldiers by the fall of 1967—is a policy which is based
upon the administration's interpretation of the nature of the Vietnam
war. The position of the administration is that the casualties, the monetary cost, the risks of a general war, the end of reconstruction of our
domestic society, and the forfeiting of the growth of international cooperation for the peaceful settlements of disputes as contained in the
United Nations Charter are costs which must be sustained because of
the nature of the war in South Vietnam.

This policy of escalation, and the costs of that policy, stem from
the interpretation by the administration of the nature of the war in
South Vietnam and the consequences of that war. Again and again,
administration spokesmen return to a basic theme to explain this war in
Vietnam: "Aggression from the North."

The White Paper on Vietnam bearing that name was issued by the
State Department on February 27, 1965. This White Paper stated
that the fighting in South Vietnam has from the start been "inspired,
directed, supplied and controlled" by North Vietnam.

The White Paper continues that "in Vietnam a Communist Government has set out deliberately to conquer a sovereign people in a

neighboring state." The record proves that "it continues to press its systematic program of armed aggression into South Vietnam." These arguments are the justification of the bombings of the North begun earlier the same month: "These strikes constitute a limited [sic] response fitted to the aggression that produced them."[1] The rationale and the policy today remain those enunciated there: "Until the regime in Hanoi decides to halt its intervention in the South . . . the United States will continue necessary measures of defense against the Communist armed aggression coming from North Viet-Nam. . . . The choice now between peace and continued and increasingly destructive conflict is one for the authorities in Hanoi to make."[2]

Here is the crucial heart of policy. Its premise is that *Aggression From the North,* to use the booklet's title, is the key factor—indeed, the sole causative factor—in the struggle in Vietnam. "Above all," it avers with emphasis, "the war in Viet-Nam is *not* a spontaneous and local rebellion against the established government. . . . In Viet-Nam a Communist government has set out deliberately to conquer a sovereign people in a neighboring state. . . ."[3] The National Liberation Front is held to be a totally subservient creature obedient to the will of its masters in Hanoi. The Viet Cong are, in effect, synonymous with North Vietnamese Communists, without whom there would be no problem. Because Hanoi is the source of all our difficulty, the war will continue until *they* yield.

I have previously set forth, paying particular attention to the details rather than to ideological generalizations, the disagreements which I and others have with this interpretation. The fighting in Vietnam in the 1960's cannot be understood outside of the context of the struggle in Vietnam in the 1940's and the 1950's. The validity of the charge of aggression from the North must be assessed against the realities of recent Vietnamese history.

Let us summarize for perspective the broad outlines of that history.

There was a genuine, popular nationalist struggle by the Vietnamese against French colonialism after World War II. For a variety of reasons, this revolution not only was nationalistic but also came to be dominated by the Vietnamese Communists led by Ho Chi Minh.

Instead of supporting the inevitable movement for Vietnamese independence from French imperialism, the United States became aligned on the side of her NATO ally, France. The United States paid as much as 80 per cent of the cost of waging this unsuccessful colonial war against the Vietnamese.

This first "Indo-Chinese War" was ended at the Geneva Conference of 1954. The Geneva Agreements made a "temporary division" of Vietnam and called for elections within two years for reunification. Despite this mandate, the Diem government refused to hold discussions on how to carry out the election and also refused to hold the election.

The Geneva Agreements specifically called the division of Vietnam into two zones a "provisional" and not a permanent division. The White Paper of 1965 refers to North Vietnam as a sovereign people. It does not deal with the negotiated settlement broken by Diem with our backing. As to two permanently "sovereign" Vietnams, the view of South Vietnamese is contained in the CBS-sponsored public opinion poll taken in South Vietnam during December 1966–January 1967. To the question, "What do you think of the reunification of North and South Vietnam when the war is over?", 83 per cent replied that they wanted "reunification very much."[4]

Another root of the fighting in the 1960's is the treatment of the South Vietnamese people by the Diem regime. As we have seen, many respected scholars characterized the Diem government as a dictatorship which alienated the bulk of the population of South Vietnam. It was this alienation and discontent which eventually led to Diem's overthrow. It was this alienation and discontent, contrary to the State Department White Paper, which created the conditions under which a Communist-led rebellion could flourish.

Although dissent from Diem was not allowed, this disaffection with Diem found expression in April 1960 in a Manifesto of eighteen non-Communist nationalist leaders. These leaders told Diem the "hard and bitter truth" that "the people do not know a better life or more freedom" under the rule of Diem.[5]

Bernard Fall succinctly stated the relationship between Diem and the fighting in the South: "Such Communist cadres will exploit occasions when they arise, but they are incapable of 'creating' a revolution from scratch. It is Diem who created the movement of discontent in South Vietnam. North Vietnam and the Vietcong fed on it."[6]

Despite the categorical denials of the White Paper of 1965, it should be impossible for any fair-minded person to dispute the fact that the fighting in the 1960's was at least partially a local rebellion against a dictatorial regime and an economic system in which a quarter of one per cent of the population owned 40 per cent of the rice land. Of course, responsible commentators do not deny that North Vietnam was supplying and assisting the N.L.F. prior to 1965 any more than they could deny that the U.S. was supplying and assisting the South Vietnamese.

Now, the crucial question which we must resolve is how we can distinguish between an indigenous rebellion which is supported from the outside and a case of armed aggression against a sovereign country. In other words, how do we determine if the charge of "aggression from the North" which prompted American escalation in 1965 was an accurate interpretation of the fighting in Vietnam?

Our own war for independence furnishes a parallel. When Cornwallis surrendered to General Washington at Yorktown, the American colonial forces were not alone. "Cornwallis was then effectively penned against salt water by sixteen thousand troops, half French and largely veterans."[7] Cornwallis could not be rescued because the French fleet was off shore preventing any British movements. One leading diplomatic historian has given this summary:

> But for those hateful rivalries [in Europe] the struggling republican colonies would not have found an ally. Great Britain would have suppressed their revolt. The French alliance, let it never be forgotten, brought independence.[8]

Anyone who would call the American War for Independence an example of aggression "supplied and controlled" from the outside (by France) would clearly be a fool. The American struggle against the British was real. The involvement and intervention of the French were also real. The American colonial revolt reveals the complexity of distinguishing between rebellion with assistance and a case of armed aggression. The White Paper of the State Department is blind to this type of complexity.

How are we to distinguish between rebellion and aggression? Once again, the arguments of the State Department are not very helpful. An earlier White Paper on Vietnam issued in 1961 asserted that

> The basic pattern of Viet Cong activity is not new, of course. It operated, with minor variations, in China, and Mao Tse-tung's theories on the conduct of guerrilla warfare are known to every Viet Cong agent and cadre. Most of the same methods were used in Malaya, in Greece, in the Philippines, in Cuba, and in Laos.[9]

Judging by this earlier White Paper, it is fair to state that the position of the State Department before 1965 was that the warfare in the South was a guerrilla warfare, comprising neither "armed aggression" nor "armed invasion." The movements to which Vietnam's guerrilla warfare was compared were primarily uprisings of local people or civil wars, not "armed aggression."

But this position was completely reversed in the 1965 White Paper.

In addition to the quotations already given, the 1965 White Paper made the absolute statements that "Vietnam is *not* another Greece . . . Vietnam is *not* another Malaya . . . Vietnam is *not* another Philippines. . . ." (Emphasis in original.)

What is the proof of "armed aggression"? How can we distinguish between a local rebellion assisted from the outside and a case of "armed aggression"? What is the evidence which caused the Department of State to change its interpretation of 1961 to the new line of "armed aggression" in 1965?

The White Paper of 1965 says that "personnel from the North, in short, are now and have always been the backbone of the entire Viet Cong operation." I. F. Stone, in his "Reply to the White Paper," wrote that "a careful reading of the text and the appendices turns up the names of only six North Vietnamese infiltrees."[10] In a public address in June 1966 the Democratic Majority Leader, Senator Mike Mansfield, called attention to the fact that "when the sharp increase in the American military effort began in early 1965, it was estimated that only about 400 North Vietnamese soldiers were among the enemy forces in the south which totalled 140,000 at that time . . .[11]

Senator Mansfield was giving the administration the benefit of the doubt. According to Secretary McNamara, information on which the estimate of "400 to 500" North Vietnamese regulars in South Vietnam was based had not been collected until March 1965.[12] This was one month after publication of the White Paper. I.F. Stone's "reply" gives a devastating analysis of the exaggeration on the case of "armed aggression." For example, a third of the State Department booklet presents the case for, and documents the origin of, Communist weapons and matériel infiltrated to the South. The treatment implies, by its space, its detailed account, and its use of language, that this is a vast operation. Without ever saying so, it gives the impression that here is the major, and criminal, source of supply which from the start has kept the Viet Cong (N.L.F.) going.

A five-page item-by-item list in an appendix details everything of Communist manufacture captured in 18 months prior to 1964, tabulated as to origin: China, Russia, Czechoslovakia, North Vietnam. Included are such items as 17 tons of potassium chlorate and 16 helmets. The total number of Communist-origin weapons in the five-page list is 179. But not reported by the State Department is the total number of *all* captured weapons against which these must be seen in perspective— 15,100 in the three years 1962, 1963, and 1964. Divide that three-year total in half, and the 18-month list of "infiltrated" weapons, far from being a major element, is less than 3 per cent of the total.

Then where do the guerrillas' weapons come from? Some are made in the "jungle factories" of the Viet Cong. But it is a fact that we ourselves were often a far bigger supplier of the enemy than Hanoi, at least until recent months. While we were capturing those 15,100 weapons, the guerrillas were capturing 27,400 from our side, for a net gain of 12,300. In 1964, just before our bombing began, the ratio was far worse from our standpoint, when in that one year South Vietnam–U.S. forces captured 4,900 weapons, only to lose 13,700. In addition to battle capture, there is enormous leakage, to theft and the black market, of almost everything in the vast stores we pour into South Vietnam, much of which ends up in Viet Cong hands. In view of these facts, which of course are not found in *Aggression From the North*, the elaborate argument to prove that "Hanoi has undertaken a program to re-equip its forces in the South with Communist-produced weapons" is simply not accurate.

More than half of the discussion of weapons supply is devoted to the discovery off South Vietnam on February 16, 1965 of a Chinese-built ship loaded with arms and munitions. But, as *The New York Times* pointed out editorially, this 100-ton vessel which is so often brought up was "not much above the Oriental junk class" in size—in fact, one World War II Liberty ship would hold 75 times as much.[13] As another comparison, a single B-52 carries more than a third the bomb tonnage such a ship could stow: eighty-four 500-pound and twenty-four 750-pound bombs, or more than 29 tons.

Walter Rostow is and has been one of the leading formulators of the administration's policy in Vietnam. In a speech in June 1961 he said, "A guerrilla war is an intimate affair, fought not merely with weapons but fought in the minds of the men who live in the villages and in the hills, fought by the spirit and policy of those who run the local government. *An outsider cannot, by himself, win a guerrilla war.*" [Italics added.][14]

This statement is an able summary of the evidence which has been presented to this point: "An outsider cannot, by himself, win a guerrilla war." My conclusion from the evidence is that the administration's interpretation of the fighting in South Vietnam as a case of "armed aggression" is a gigantic fairy tale.

Echoing the theme of the 1965 White Paper, Secretary Rusk said on October 12, 1967, "We did not put our combat forces into South

Vietnam because of dissident elements in South Vietnam. We put our combat forces in there because North Vietnamese forces moved into South Vietnam. So that our problem of peace is with Hanoi."[15]

Pure fairy tale. The White Paper documents only six North Vietnamese infiltrators in South Vietnam at the end of 1964. According to the figures of Secretary McNamara, which were compiled one month after the White Paper was issued, there were 400 to 500 North Vietnamese troops in South Vietnam. During this same period, there were already over 20,000 American troops in South Vietnam.

The fact is that the administration did put American troops in, did escalate the war, precisely because of the success of the dissident element inside of South Vietnam. Of course the Viet Cong were assisted from the North. Of course Hanoi did respond to the American escalation with a similar escalation by sending regular North Vietnamese units into South Vietnam. But this "armed aggression" was the *result* of the administration's policy, not the *cause* of it.

Let us look back over events leading to the introduction of American troops in 1965 which was based at that time upon the charge of "armed aggression."

In March 1964 Secretary McNamara candidly admitted that "the situation in South Vietnam has unquestionably worsened."[16] McNamara spoke of the gains of the Viet Cong and "the large indigenous support that the Viet Cong receives." Although concerned, McNamara was optimistic. He stated that "we have high hopes" for the new government of General Khanh.

> Today the government of General Khanh is vigorously re-building the machinery of administration and reshaping plans to carry the war to the Viet Cong. He is an able and energetic leader. He has demonstrated his grasp of the basic elements . . . required to defeat the Viet Cong. He is planning a program of economic and social advances for the welfare of his people. . . .

The Secretary continued that we could become more involved only as "a supplement to, not a substitute for, progress within South Vietnam's own borders."[17]

Both the Secretary's analysis of the government of Khanh and his prognosis for the future administration course were more fairy tales. Internal conditions in South Vietnam continued to deteriorate and the administration decided to intervene to substitute American boys for the failures of the South Vietnamese in order to prevent the total overthrow of the Saigon government by the Viet Cong. In other words, the rationale for America is exactly the opposite of the one stated by Secretary Rusk in October 1967. It is exactly the opposite of the charge of "armed aggression" by outsiders.

Bernard Fall called the fighting between the Viet Cong, assisted by North Vietnam, and the Saigon army, assisted by the United States, the "Second Indo-Chinese War." Douglas Pike, who served for six years as a foreign service officer with the United States Information Agency in Saigon, stated in his study, *Viet Cong*, that this second war ended in 1965 when the Viet Cong were on the threshold of victory and the Johnson administration decided to commit United States troops to prevent it. According to Pike, another and different war began in 1965.[18]

In order to formulate policy we must, as I have said, see the "realities" of South Vietnam—the way out of the American involvement can be based only upon these realities. Perhaps the central argument of this book rests upon the fact that *a policy of escalation has produced conditions which appear to verify the original justification for that escalation.*

In other words, when Rusk said in his October 1967 news conference that "there are North Vietnamese regiments fighting in South Vietnam"[19] he obviously is absolutely right. From this Rusk draws a justification of the use of American troops in Vietnam because Hanoi had placed North Vietnamese troops in South Vietnam. But this position is absolutely false. According to the evidence in the 1965 White Paper and our analysis of the roots of the fighting in the 1960's, it is clear that prior to 1965 the fighting in South Vietnam was primarily a local rebellion, a revolution, being supported on the one side by the United States and on the other by North Vietnam. In the words of Presidential advisor Rostow, "an outsider cannot, by himself, win a guerrilla war."

In 1965, when the local guerrilla forces supported from the outside were nearing victory, the administration, contrary to its position in the 1964 election, decided to substitute American boys to do the job that Asian boys had failed to do.

The Americanization of the war in Vietnam cannot bring about progress or a solution because *we* cannot give progress or a solution to the South Vietnamese. By this I mean exactly what the formulators of the administration's policy—the McNamaras, the Rusks, the Rostows, the Bundys—have always said but have never practiced: only the South Vietnamese can build a South Vietnam that will win the loyalty of the people of South Vietnam.

If the "problem" in Vietnam were really outside aggression, as the most powerful nation in the world the United States would be able to defeat an outside aggressor and thus solve the "problem." But this is not the nature of the conflict in Vietnam or the way out. We cannot make the people loyal to the Saigon regime any more than we could make them loyal to Diem or the French before Diem. The engagement of the world's greatest power has not changed the "realities" in Vietnam now any more than it could fourteen years ago when a young Senator arose in his place to address his colleagues. "Mr. President," he began, "the time has come for the American people to be told the blunt truth about Indo-China."

I have a mimeographed copy of that speech, somewhat yellowed with age. Some of its sentences are underlined for emphasis. Among them are these, which might have been spoken yesterday in the same place.

"To pour our money, matériel and men into the jungles of Indo-China without at least a remote prospect of victory would be dangerously futile and self-destructive. . . . Despite (a) series of optimistic reports about eventual victory, every member of the Senate knows that such victory today appears to be desperately remote, to say the least, despite tremendous amounts of economic and material aid from the United States, and despite a deplorable loss of . . . manpower. . . . I am frankly of the belief that no amount of American military assistance can conquer an enemy which is everywhere and at the same time nowhere, 'an enemy of the people' which has the sympathy and covert support of the people." The day Senator John F. Kennedy voiced those views was April 6, 1954.[20]

Marvin L. Stone of the *U.S. News and World Report* staff, in a remarkable 12-page article captioned "Is U.S. Trapped in a 'Hopeless War'?" in the magazine's December 5, 1966 issue, has a graphic description of the guerrilla: "He lives in the area where he fights. He is comfortable in the dark. He has motivation. He is a hard man to find, living anonymously in the midst of his fellow countrymen. As soon as he puts his rifle back in its plastic cover and slips it under the dike of his rice field, he is undistinguishable from the others."[21]

Most accounts agree that the Viet Cong are firm believers in their cause, patriots in their own view, with a dedication to whatever hardship must be endured in order to survive and overcome. "Many American officers," says one *New York Times* account, "consider them the wiliest, most tenacious enemies ever faced by the United States."[22]

But among Saigon government troops there is a noticeable contrast in dedication, ability, and willingness. A study prepared by General Westmoreland's staff, taking a detailed look at the Vietnamese army, was reported in December 1966 to be "critical of virtually every phase of the army's operations." The main problem was said to be poor leadership at every level, with officer selection based almost entirely on education rather than leadership ability. Promotions are apt to depend more on political favoritism and loyalty to superiors than on ability. There has been no opportunity whatever for ordinary soldiers and noncommissioned men to rise to officer rank. The average young officer, fresh out of school, does not even speak the dialect of his peasant troops, whom he looks down upon. In a country still filled with mandarin tradition, his middle-class status and his position as a "baccalaureate" help him see himself as a privileged character. Some, says Marvin Stone, still insist on being served tea in bed in the morning.

A private, who may be drafted for three years at $23 a month, is paid less than a housemaid in Saigon. He is supposed to provide his own rations out of an allowance of 20 cents a day, which may actually shrink to as little as 5 cents by the time it filters down to him. Although it is supposed to be forbidden, troops on missions through the countryside frequently help themselves to whatever they find available for food; the practice has been one factor in turning the countryside against the Saigon government. Ward Just, accompanying Vietnamese infantry on a "search-and-destroy" mission in the Delta—men from a division "generally considered the finest Division in the Vietnamese army"— has given a vivid description which illustrates why the South Vietnamese are not winning the war against the guerrillas.[23]

The mission began at 5 A.M. with six armored personnel carriers moving out from the Baclieu airfield, "collecting infantrymen along the way from their houses, as a school bus collects children." Moving through rice fields and up to treelines, they would dismount, look in huts and search for foxholes. At one point they found fresh foxholes and a trail the Viet Cong had presumably taken after spending the night. But instead of following it, they piled back in their carriers. "Everyone was hungry," says the report, by the time the sixty or so men stopped outside three houses. Earlier, in some of their stops, they had picked up some eggs and some greens; one man had fired his carbine at a flock of birds. Now "three or four .30-caliber machine gun rounds were squeezed off into the pigsty, frightening the pigs and scattering them." Later a woman with two tiny children, one of them naked, came out of one of the huts and went down to count the pigs, none of which was taken. Ward Just gives no explanation for the machine-gun firing—was it just an irresponsible soldier in sadistic play? Or was it a deliberate "softening up" of the residents for what was to come? After the pigsty incident

. . . the men poured out of the tractors and raced toward the houses. One private, a crayfish in one hand and his carbine in the other, lurched after a duck in a pond. He dropped the carbine, got the duck, strangled it, and put it in a burlap sack.

Another emerged from a hut, his helmet full of eggs. Another seized a 20-pound bag of rice. A third was catching chickens and plucking and washing them. A fourth was building the fire.

Inside one hut, an old man and his wife watched the feast grow. A sergeant was interrogating them as his men moved in and out of the hut, taking plates. . . . The booty inside the APC's (armored personnel carriers) grew until they resembled Noah's arks, each machine laden with three or four chickens or ducks, mostly chickens. . . .

The commonest complaints of the Americans who serve as advisors to the Vietnamese units (over which they have little command control) are, in addition to lack of leadership, harshness toward the civilian population, such as this incident illustrates; corruption; and lack of aggressiveness.

The plain truth is that the average South Vietnamese, whether soldier or civilian, just doesn't care. He is not fighting for a cause he has any feeling about, as are the Viet Cong. The result is that "South Vietnamese, by and large, seem to be spectators at their own war."[24] As to the military, all too often (although many units have performed well) incidents occur such as that in which the commander of a Regional Forces unit north of Saigon upon losing one man to a sniper's bullet turned his unit around and marched it to the rear. A young commander in the Delta, questioned about the apparent unwillingness of his troops to engage the enemy, declared that "the most important thing in war is to keep all of your troops alive." Where a U.S. patrol of nine men will go out at night on "ambush patrol," says one American, "these young South Vietnamese officers won't go out with less than two full companies—200 men. And you feel they would do almost anything to avoid contact."[25] An American battalion commander, flanked by three different Vietnamese battalions over a period of several weeks, found one of them satisfactory; a second, alerted for a surprise attack in six hours, took thirty-six hours to get ready, delaying on every pretext until the Viet Cong had long since departed; and the third battalion "just decided to bug out in the dead of night. Never said a word to us—just hauled their tails out of there. The VC could have moved into the hole and clobbered us."[26]

Thus the war effort has become increasingly Americanized because the South Vietnamese have failed their tasks. Administration spokesmen, like McNamara in his view of the Khanh government, always have "high hopes" for the next Saigon regime. When this fairy tale is smashed by reality, more Americans are called upon to do the tasks for the Vietnamese.

One general has commented, "Every time Westy makes a speech about how good the South Vietnam Army is, I want to ask him why he keeps calling for more Americans. His need for reinforcements is a measure of our failure with the Vietnamese."[27] Americans cannot solve Vietnam's problems for the South Vietnamese.

An American who had worked in the provinces of South Vietnam for over five years put forward the same opinion by the use of an allegory: "Nobody considers the Viet Cong Robin Hood any more. But the government and the army are still the Sheriff of Nottingham, and you'll never sell that."[28]

Veteran *Washington Post* correspondent Ward Just is also aware that "the war can only be won by the Vietnamese." Because of this awareness, and because of his experiences which convinced him that "the level of leadership, both in Saigon and in the provinces, is low," he arrived at the following painful conclusions: "This war is not being won, and by any reasonable estimate, it is not going to be won in the foreseeable future. It may be unwinnable."[29]

Sir Robert Thompson, a leading British authority on counterinsurgency who is generally friendly to the administration, wrote in September 1967 that the policies of the administration "smack more of desperation than of resolution." He does not believe that these "desperate measures" offer a solution to the problems in South Vietnam.[30]

Americans cannot solve Vietnam's problems for the South Vietnamese. Since the administration has not comprehended the nature of the conflict in Vietnam as it really was before 1965, the policy they have devised does not offer a solution to the problems of Vietnam or a way out of this morass. In the words of Sir Robert Thompson, this leads to "desperate . . . hasty and temporary stop-gap policies."

When *New York Times* correspondent Neil Sheehan went to Vietnam in 1962, he felt that he "believed in what my country was doing in Vietnam." When he left after his second tour in 1966 he concluded: "I was naive in believing the non-Communist Vietnamese could defeat the Communist insurgency and build a decent and progressive social structure." Why didn't the Saigon regimes achieve social progress? Sheehan wrote that substantive measures for reform suggested by Americans "have been sabotaged because the regimes were and are composed of men who are members of, or who are allied with, mandarin families that hold title to properties they have no intention of renouncing."[31]

Americans cannot solve South Vietnam's problems for the Vietnamese. Flailing an aggressor has not changed the realities in South Vietnam. As under the French, as under Diem, as under Diem's successors, the bulk of the people have no reason to fight for or support the Saigon regime.

South Vietnam was able to carry out a national election in September 1967 that gave legitimacy to the government of General Thieu and Marshal Ky. This is a commendable exercise. However, I do not have "high hopes" that this exercise will advance the cause of progress in South Vietnam.

Why do I hold this position? The government of Ky and Thieu had been in power for over two years before the election. During that period, America escalated the war in order to compensate for South Vietnamese failures. During that period, there were no fundamental social reforms undertaken on behalf of the Vietnamese people.

I hold this position, this lack of "high hopes," because, as *The New York Times* has said editorially, "Saigon's failure is precisely that it has not given the country anything to fight for, apart from the negative slogan of anti-communism. The thorough overhaul of South Vietnamese society that is urgently required is nowhere in sight, despite the lip service Premier Ky and General Thieu have long paid to reform."[32]

It was the failures of the Saigon regime plus the involved struggle in Vietnam since the end of World War II that provided the discontent on which the Viet Cong and the North Vietnamese fed. When these failures increased, the power of the Viet Cong increased. At that point, the administration substituted American soldiers for South Vietnamese soldiers, and the North Vietnamese also escalated the war.

We cannot allow the *results* of the policy of escalation to obscure our vision of the *causes* of the policy of escalation. The index of American escalation is the index of South Vietnamese failure. The Americanization of the war effort in the South cannot reverse the weaknesses and the failings of a succession of Saigon regimes. Nor can the bombing of the North solve the fundamental problem of eradicating the social diseases on which the guerrilla war in the South thrives.

VII

Bombing the North

The strikes at a railroad yard and truck depot in the Hanoi area on December 13 and 14, 1966, at a time when Pope Paul and others were urging a new bombing pause and increased peace efforts, brought a Radio Hanoi charge that we had killed or wounded more than 100 civilians. From Saigon, General Westmoreland's command said categorically that of our bombs "none fell in the city of Hanoi."

When State Department spokesman Robert McCloskey was asked, "Have we bombed Hanoi?" he answered similarly, "We have not." But after a pause he asked, "What do you mean by Hanoi?" It turned out that our targets had been described as five and six miles from a "zero point" near the heart of the city, not from city limits. "Let New Yorkers," said *The New York Times* editorially, "ponder whether their city was being bombed if a five-mile circle drawn around Times Square was left untouched but targets just outside were hit."[1]

The greatest credibility crisis of the bombing war in the North might have passed as one more conflict between Hanoi propaganda and official U.S. denials. But then *The New York Times'* Pulitzer prize-winner and Assistant Managing Editor, Harrison E. Salisbury, with a previous State Department clearance, was unexpectedly given a visa by Hanoi and flew in on an International Control Commission plane from Phnom Penh, Cambodia.

Salisbury documented the fact that American bombing in the North, contrary to the statements of the administration, had produced substantial civilian casualties and destroyed numerous civilian dwellings.[*] Similar reports had been previously made by European and other non-Communist correspondents who had visited North Vietnam, only to be ignored or discounted in the United States. However, now there was a renowned American source, Salisbury, giving eye-witness accounts of civilian bomb damage which previously had been repeatedly denied by the administration. Salisbury's articles momentarily aroused the slumbering conscience and sensitivities of the nation.

His dispatches told of 13 houses destroyed three minutes from his hotel and 100 yards from the central market; of 300 thatch and brick homes and huts "leveled by blast and fire" not much farther away; of the suburb of Phuxa four miles from the city's center with 24 houses destroyed in an August raid; of October raids on Phu Ly, a town of 10,000 35 miles from Saigon, where "every house and building was destroyed"; of "block after block of utter desolation" as viewed from the cathedral tower of Nam Dinh, a textile center and North Vietnam's third largest city (95,000 population, cut to 20,000 by evacuation), hit by 51 raids since June 28, 1965.

"Whatever the explanation," he wrote, "one can see that United States planes are dropping an enormous weight of explosives on purely civilian targets. . . . President Johnson's announced policy that American targets in North Vietnam are steel and concrete rather than human lives seems to have little connection with the reality of attacks carried out by United States planes." "It is the conviction of the North Vietnamese that the United States is deliberately directing bombs against the civilian population although ostensibly contending that 'military objectives' are the target."[2]

With such evidence attested to by an unimpeachable American reporter, charges of civilian destruction could no longer be dismissed as Hanoi's propaganda. After lame explanations that returning anti-aircraft flak, or perhaps surface-to-air missiles falling back or running wild, could have been responsible for North Vietnam's civilian damage, it was finally acknowledged by administration officials on December 26 that "American pilots had accidentally struck civilian areas in North Vietnam

[*]   *Dr. Louis Betz, an American working in the Hoian provincial hospital, told Senator Edward Kennedy there that "half the civilian war casualties were caused by the Viet Cong and half by the allies." (The New York Times, January 6, 1968, p. 8.) American bombing in the South is probably more destructive to civilian life and property than in the North.*

while attempting to bomb military targets" and that "It is impossible to avoid all damage to civilian areas."[3]

Thus a new dimension of the war in the North was revealed.

An earlier report on civilian bombing in the North was that of foreign editor Minoru Omori of the seven-million-circulation Japanese newspaper *Mainichi* (*Daily News*). In a dispatch dated October 2, 1965 he describes viewing in Hanoi a documentary film reported to have been made by North Vietnam's National Motion Picture Department between July 12 and 22, 1965, when our planes in ten successive days of raids are said to have destroyed 150 buildings in a 2,300-patient leprosarium at Quynh Lap in Nge An province, killing 139 and wounding 80.

"The screen," he wrote in *Mainichi's* English edition, "showed medical supplies scattered all over the place, Red Cross flags torn to shreds, hospitals whose roofs were blown off, hospital rooms with walls gone and half destroyed beds under heaps of rubble." Some of the scenes, taken by photographers rushed to the spot after the first bombing, caught dramatic action. "Patients on crutches are seen running helter-skelter, the nurses trying to take refuge in shelters carrying on their backs patients who are unable to walk. Among the patients trying to run for their lives are small children and aged persons. And suddenly in their midst the bombs and napalms explode spreading fire and death. . . . I have never seen such an appalling film."

In concluding his account, Omori says: "The film showed that the American planes flew at a considerably low altitude. It could be possible that the planes mistook the hospitals for military barracks. But the planes should have noticed the Red Cross marks on the roofs.

"Until I reached Hanoi, I trusted the American conscience and believed that the targets of their bombings were limited to the military installations. I deeply regret what I have to report."[4] Our Japanese embassy denied that we had "deliberately" bombed the leprosarium.[5]

At supersonic speeds, and under such intense fire, our planes are bound to make errors, whether at high altitudes where targets are hard to hit, or at low levels where they flash past in an instant only. It is only natural to seek to compensate by dropping huge quantities of bombs in the hope that the law of averages will put some squarely on target. Even in South Vietnam, unprotected by such withering anti-aircraft fire, our planes have made numerous reported "mistakes" in bombing innocent civilians and even our own South Vietnamese forces.

Near the end of World War II in Europe, President Roosevelt established the Strategic Bombing Survey, an eleven-man civilian board

79

charged with responsibility for a comprehensive inquiry into the effect of bombing in Germany. Based in London, the survey employed 300 civilians and 850 military personnel.[6]

One finding dealt with bombing accuracy. "As for the vaunted precision bombing of our air forces," commented Alan Barth of the *Washington Post*, and now its chief editorial writer, "the same report discloses that 'while accuracy improved during the war, in the overall, only about 20 percent of the bombs aimed at precision targets fell within the target area.'"[7]

Has accuracy improved in Vietnam? "It took 11 missions by 40 airplanes last week," wrote Ward Just from Saigon in September 1966, "to destroy a 50-car freight train near Hanoi. It was traveling on a track frequently and devastatingly hit by bombers, and yet it was still able to function, in part."[8] Senator Stuart Symington, a former Air Force Secretary, has noted a similar bridge situation: "I saw pictures of a bridge. The Navy said they had hit it twice. The Air Force said they had tried three times. We lost two pilots and two planes, and the bridge looks about as good as the day it was built."[9]

As the scope and intensity of the bombing in the North increased, the effects on the civilian population increased. In August 1967, many American papers ran pictures taken by the *Agence France-Press* showing extensive damage in residential sections of Hanoi. In response, *The New York Times* commented editorially: "The stuttering flow of explanations was the price paid for past lack of candor on the inevitability of some civilian deaths in any bombing of urban areas. But at least the vehemence of the effort to explain indicated Washington's concern for holding civilian casualties to a minimum, plus an uneasiness of conscience over inadvertent exceptions to the rule. The French news dispatches from Hanoi, with their companion pictures of rubble and flattened houses near a central market place, suggest that even these restraints are now being abandoned. The Pentagon may again assert that only military targets have been attacked, but there seems no way of reconciling the bomb damage in the heart of North Vietnam's capital with the stated policy of 'avoiding populated areas.'"[10]

On August 29, 1967, David Schoenbrunn, a former correspondent for CBS, reported from Hanoi that he had seen at least ten bodies pulled from the rubble of a block of shops and apartments in the center of Hanoi, a few blocks from a hotel where foreigners are quartered. He continued that "some 150 foreign diplomats, delegations and journalists witnessed the scene Tuesday, August 22 when a 500-kilo (1,000-pound) bomb hit the heart of the residential section. Extensive damage was done to an eye-ear-throat clinic, with one doctor and one medical aide killed and several nurses injured."[11]

Given the evidence from the eye-witness accounts, given the impossibility of precision bombing, the conclusion is undeniable that bombing the North has yielded a far greater loss of civilian life and property than the administration has been willing to reveal to the American people. This damage to civilians is one of the costs of the air war. It must be included, not excluded, in making our judgment whether the results of this policy are greater than the costs and the risks. We must not practice the same moral insensitivity as do the other participants in this bloody conflict. If the costs of bombing the North are in fact greater than the benefits, this policy should be abandoned. As the *Washington Post* commented, "To achieve great military purposes, some loss of civilian life might be tolerated, but if nothing is being gained and civilians are being killed, the case for stopping the bombing is almost irresistible."[12]

In order to decide if bombing the North is a worthwhile policy, we should determine if the bombing will: break the will of the people and government of the North; "force" the D.R.V. to the negotiating table; end or reduce substantially the flow of necessary supplies to the South; in sum, raise the costs, in the terminology of Secretary McNamara, to such a height that the North Vietnamese will be willing to submit to the American terms. Let us now turn to an investigation of these questions.

The conclusion reached by the Strategic Bombing survey said: "The city attacks of the R.A.F. prior to the autumn of 1944 did not substantially affect the course of German war production. German war production as a whole continued to increase."[13] This bombing was unlimited and against a highly industrialized economy. The contrast with North Vietnam on these two conditions is well known. Can the bombing of North Vietnam produce more effective results?

The evidence shows, in the first place, that our tremendous quantity of explosives, dropped at vast cost, has a relatively small effect. Hanson W. Baldwin, the military editor of *The New York Times*, has said: "There is no doubt that much of the tonnage is wasted on green and uninhabited jungle. When the target is one truck, as it often is, there are bound to be many misses."[14]

In North Vietnam there are few large targets, and consequently there have been questions raised as to the value of the objectives given to pilots. "I recall one mission of three aircraft," writes former Navy pilot Norde Wilson, holder of an Air Medal with nine clusters after two

Vietnam tours, "on which we were directed to make three passes each, to destroy two small water wheels on a stream in the middle of nowhere. Ten million dollars in equipment and six highly skilled aviators, being utilized for a valueless target of this nature . . . [which] might be reported in the States as one irrigation plant destroyed."[15]

An Air Force officer, writing to the magazine *Aviation Week*, comments similarly on the inflated terms used to describe such insignificant targets. "When an article reads 'structures destroyed,' " he says, "the definition means a straw-thatched hut. 'Boat' means anything from a 12-ft. one-man dugout to slightly larger sampans. 'Bridge' means a bamboo foot-bridge or a pair of logs felled across a stream. . . . To be sure, these targets must be hit to keep 'Charlie' on the run, but at such cost? . . . A VC hutch is worth at most $20; a pack animal, maybe $100; a bridge, the sweat to fell a few trees. . . ."[16] A napalm bomb, he notes, costs $300, and the 250-pound Mark 81, $250; heavier bombs, of course, are more costly. A single round of 20-mm. ammunition is $2.45, and we have aircraft capable of firing up to 6,000 such rounds—nearly $15,000 worth—in one minute.

Ward Just, noting the vast numbers of bridges reported destroyed in North Vietnam, tried to find out how many bridges there actually are. "How many could there be if they were being destroyed at the rate of 133 a week?" He found no one to give him an answer, but military officials pointed out that the North Vietnamese are "amazingly adept" at repairing damaged bridges, and that to destroy a bridge a direct hit must explode on the bridge itself. "Often the bombs go through the bridge and explode relatively harmlessly underneath it."[17]

Frequent use of pontoon bridges has been reported by our fliers and reconnaissance. North Vietnam claims that there are more bridges now than ever before, including some where ferries used to serve. The floating bridges are described as having a roadway supported by huge bundles of unsinkable bamboo, built in easily transportable and joinable sections. They can be assembled quickly at nightfall, towed away at daybreak, and reassembled next evening at any one of a dozen or so crossing points to which new branch roads of the main highway now lead.

The pre-planning technique, Salisbury reports, has been used also in highway and rail repair, with "repair materials probably sufficient to construct two or three additional railroads . . . kept on hand, seldom more than a few hundred yards from any possible break." If rail damage is severe enough, temporary new tracks are simply laid to bypass the section and trains are soon running again. Highway repair materials and manpower are "stockpiled in advance, apparently along the whole expanse of Route 1."

Even if mechanized transport could be cut out entirely, there are still animal and human means available requiring no fuel. Even bicycles, says Baldwin, are among our targets.[18] He does not say why, but several published pictures, including one released by the Associated Press, show a line of bicycles adapted for transport stretching down the road as far as can be seen. Broad shelves built out two or three feet on each side are piled to saddle level the length of the frame with burdens. Because of the load, the "riders"—uniformed and helmeted in one such picture—are walking, apparently providing motive power with a sort of pump-handle lever rising above the rear wheel and steering with a long extension attached to the left handlebar. Says an account in the *Washington Star*: "One sees columns over a mile long, every bicycle loaded with an average of 550 pounds of supplies, wheeled an average of 20 miles a day, mainly along secondary roads."[19]

General Matthew Ridgway, who commanded the United Nations forces in Korea, has said that Korea "taught that it is impossible to interdict the supply routes of an Asian army by air power alone. . . . Unquestionably, we inflicted serious damage upon the Chinese and greatly complicated their problems of reinforcement and supply. But we did not halt their offensive nor materially diminish its strength." The reason was that they operated much as do the Vietnamese: "The Chinese, like the Vietnamese, traveled light, with each man carrying his ammunition, his food and his weapon on his back. They moved at night or on hidden footpaths and goat tracks, immune from air attack."[20]

It is evident that we have not stopped or substantially reduced infiltration of men and supplies by bombing the North. As noted earlier, the rate of entry into the South went up from 1,500 men per month to 4,500 per month between the start of our bombing, in February 1965, and the end of the year—and up again to 7,000–8,000 per month by the end of 1966. Thus, the second of our three objectives—we did achieve the bolstering of morale in the South for a time, for whatever it was worth—that of cutting off the southward flow, has not been won. It is dubious whether it can be. As to the third objective, that of breaking North Vietnam's morale and bringing her to the peace table, the possibility appears equally remote.

Although the continental United States has never experienced enemy bombing attacks during a war, the psychological impact of bombing on civilians should not be difficult to comprehend. Instead of their reacting according to Secretary McNamara's quantitative-oriented analysis of increasing the costs and therefore decreasing the will, or according to General Westmoreland's dictum that the enemy's "rate of decline will be in proportion to the pressure directed against him," the anger, the determination, and the will to resist of a people under bombardment is increased. As we should be aware from the experience of the Britons in World War II, the bombing of civilians hardened rather than softened the attitude of the people.

Salisbury, as well as other outside observers in North Vietnam, has seen that the North Vietnamese people have undergone this very predictable reaction. A full year before Salisbury made his reports, James Cameron, the well-respected and reliable British journalist, wrote from his observations in Hanoi that "if the bombing of North Vietnam is designed either to terrorize the people into submission or crush their economy into ruin, its effect on both counts is precisely the reverse." Cameron continued that the effect of the bombing was to stimulate and consolidate the people behind the policy of the government.[21]

The effect of the bombing on the "will" of the people has not changed since Cameron's report in December 1965. As recently as August 1967, Mr. Schoenbrunn cited evidence that "the bombing has yielded them major political, psychological and social gains, creating a hard-line unity in the civilian population."[22]

Second, we are dealing with a rural-based and not an industrialized country, one which can absorb our heaviest blows with a great deal of resilience. As Bernard Fall put it, "Primitiveness carries its own kind of invulnerability." In addition, many of the sinews of war are supplied from outside, from China and Russia: anti-aircraft guns and missiles, construction manpower, MIG fighters such as the additional one hundred supplied by Russia in December 1966, ammunition, "more radar sets per square mile than in Eastern Europe."[23] This source of supply we cannot touch without risk of World War III.

As a matter of fact, we are constantly running those risks anyway as we escalate the war in the North. On June 19, 1967 the Pentagon admitted (after a prior denial) that American planes had hit a Soivet freighter docked at a North Vietnamese port. In August 1967 targets less than a minute's flying time from China were bombed and in the same month two American planes were shot down inside China.

The administration continues to argue that neither China nor Russia will intervene beyond furnishing supplies as long as the United States does not threaten China, Russia, or the existence of North Vietnam. But this is only wishful thinking.

It must be clearly understood that these incidents could provoke a Chinese or a Russian response. There can be no guarantee of the reaction of the other side. The American people must realize that the actions of the administration can be viewed as serious provocations by certain factions within the government of Russia and China. Therefore, it is fair to say that the decision for the initiation of World War III is entirely outside of our control and lies in the hands of the present or future governments in Peking and Moscow. The tragedy of this predicament, as *The New York Times* noted in connection with the escalation of the bombing, is that "there is no evidence that this heightened risk-taking will either curb Hanoi's war effort in South Vietnam or diminish its will to fight."

My own conclusion that continued bombing of the North should be terminated is supported by results of a survey prepared by the Central Intelligence Agency and the Pentagon's Defense Intelligence Agency. Details are classified, but the general conclusions were discussed in the press in December 1966.

Richard Dudman, *St. Louis Post-Dispatch* Washington correspondent, wrote that the survey "has concluded that the American bombing of North Vietnam is a political and military failure. . . . On the political side, the survey is said to find that the bombing has clearly failed to accomplish its major objective—to inflict sufficient punishment on North Vietnam to persuade it to stop supporting the war in the South or go further and seek peace talks. Militarily, the air attacks have failed to impede significantly the growing stream of men and supplies from North Vietnam into the South, the survey is said to show."[24]

In 1966 I had proposed publicly that a civilian commission along the lines of the Strategic Bombing Survey be established to appraise the effectiveness of our bombing policy. I thought that such a group would substantiate the data and conclusions presented in this chapter. Perhaps the authority of such a group could have helped to bring an end to the bombing which is sought by me and others.

Since that time, precisely such an authoritative judgment on the effectiveness of the bombing has been made available to the American people. This is the detailed statement given by Defense Secretary McNamara on August 25, 1967 in testimony before the Preparedness Subcommittee of the Senate Armed Services Committee. As *The New York Times* commented: "Secretary McNamara's devastating counterattack against the victory-through-airpower lobby destroys the myth that expanded bombing of North Vietnam could win the war, but it does far more than that. Indirectly—but inescapably—it undermines the administration's own argument that suspension of the bombing is too high a price to pay to bring Hanoi to the negotiating table."[25]

I believe that the facts contained in McNamara's statement prove beyond the shadow of a doubt the fruitlessness, the hopelessness, the ineffectiveness, the total bankruptcy of the policy of bombing the North. Because these facts must be comprehended if we are to follow a policy in Vietnam which is in the national interest, a lengthy excerpt from McNamara's testimony is warranted.

"Complete interdiction of these supplies," he said, "has never been considered possible by our military leaders. . . . Our experience in Korea demonstrated the unlikelihood that air strikes or other means could choke off the minimum amounts needed to support enemy forces. . . . Moreover, it should be noted that the geography of the infiltration routes is less favorable to interdiction than was the case in Korea. . . .

"[North Vietnam] had no real war-making industrial base and hence none which would be destroyed by bombing. . . . Unfortunately for the chances of effective interdiction, this simple agricultural economy has a highly diversified transportation system consisting of rails and roads and waterways. The North Vietnamese use barges and sampans, trucks and foot power, and even bicycles capable of carrying 500-pound loads to move goods over this network. The capacity of this system is large— the volume of traffic it is now required to carry, in relation to its capacity, is small. . . .

"Intelligence estimates suggest that the quantity of externally supplied material, other than food, required to support the VC/NVA forces in South Vietnam at about their current level of combat activity is very, very small. The reported figure is significantly 15 tons per day, but even if the quantity were five times that amount it could be transported by only a few trucks. . . .

"There is no basis to believe that any bombing campaign, short of one which had population as its target, would by itself force Ho Chi Minh's regime into submission. . . . There are only 57 targets recommended by the Joint Chiefs of Staff against which strikes have not yet been authorized. Whatever the merits of striking these 57 targets may be, I believe it is clear that strikes against them will not materially shorten the war. . . .

"As to breaking their will, I have seen no evidence in any of the many intelligence reports that would lead me to believe that a less selective bombing campaign would change the resolve of the North Vietnamese leaders or deprive them of the support of the North Vietnamese people. . . . Perhaps most important of all, the people of North Vietnam are accustomed to discipline and are no strangers to deprivation and to death. Available information indicates that, despite some war weariness, they remain willing to endure hardship and they continue to respond to the direction of the Hanoi regime. There is little reason to believe that any level of conventional air or naval action, short of sustained and systematic bombing of the population centers, will deprive the North Vietnamese of their willingness to continue to support their Government's efforts. . . .

"There is also nothing in the past reaction of the North Vietnamese leaders that would provide any confidence that they can be bombed to the negotiating table. . . . The course of conflict on the ground in the south, rather than the scale of air attack in the north, appears to be the determining factor in North Vietnam's willingness to continue. . . .

"But the capacity of the lines of communication and of the outside sources of supply so far exceed the minimal flow necessary to support the present level of North Vietnamese military effort in South Vietnam that the enemy operations in the South cannot, on the basis of any reports I have seen, be stopped by air bombardment—short, that is, of the virtual annihilation of North Vietnam and its people. . . .

"As I have mentioned, estimates of the total tonnage required start at 15 tons per day of nonfood supplies. This can be quintupled and still be dwarfed by North Vietnam's actual imports of about 5,800 tons per day. And its import capacity is much greater. The ports together with the roads and railroads from China have an estimated capacity of about 14,000 tons a day. . . .

"Haiphong represents the easiest and cheapest means of import. If it and the other ports were to be closed, and on the unrealistic assumption that closing the ports would eliminate all seaborne imports, North Vietnam would still be able to import over 8,400 tons a day by rail, road, and waterway. . . . It seems obvious that cutting off seaborne imports would not prevent North Vietnam from continuing its present level of military operations in the south.

"Elimination of Haiphong and the two other ports as a source of supply would not in fact eliminate seaborne imports."[26]

The policy of bombing the North has not been effective or productive. McNamara's testimony reveals that there is no hope that this policy is any more likely to be productive in the future.

On the other hand, there is every reason to believe that a suspension of the bombing would be followed by direct peace talks between the D.R.V. and the United States. The administration was assured by Russian leaders in February 1967, by U Thant, by other Western, non-aligned, and Eastern European sources, and by the North Vietnamese that a suspension of the bombing would be followed by direct discussions.

By continuing an unproductive, indeed a counter-productive, policy of bombing the North, the administration is maintaining the major road block in the path to the conference table. Given the fruitlessness of this policy as documented in the McNamara testimony, given the hopelessness of bombing the North as a method of getting the D.R.V. to the conference table, there is every reason to test the assurances we have been given, to suspend the bombing and wait for the peace talks to begin. The simple fact that no negotiations will begin while the United States is bombing the D.R.V. is the central argument for abandoning this risk-filled and barren policy.

It is a sad commentary that instead of suspending the bombing, instead of even backing the limits on escalation implied by McNamara, the attacks on new targets in August and September 1967 substantiate the comment of George Wilson in the *Washington Post* that "it appears from the outside that the President is now taking the military's advice over McNamara's. . . ."[27] Announcement of Secretary McNamara's resignation to head the World Bank seemed to many to confirm such a judgment.

VIII

The Third War in Vietnam

"There are really three wars raging in Vietnam. There is a military war, a political war, and an economic war. Without victory in the last, success in the other two would be meaningless."

—*The Moss report**

Mr. Nguyen (not his real name) is deputy director of a key Saigon ministry dealing with personnel problems of the South Vietnam government's 120,000 civil servants. He is himself a top-ranking official, a man trained in French universities, diplomas from which adorn his office walls. Unlike many government employees, he devotes a full official day to his work. His pay was the third highest in his ministry in February 1966: $100 per month. Yet Mr. Nguyen, as befits a French-educated upper-level government employee, supports four children in private schools, occasionally buys his wife some jewelry, and wears a clean white shirt every day. His expenses run to $350 a month, more than triple his salary. How does he do it?

The answer is through his "outside interests," pursued in his case after conscientious office hours. As a used car dealer, he buys automobiles from Americans leaving the country and sells them to wealthy Vietnamese at a 50 to 100 per cent profit. To pay the Americans in

---

*   *See footnote 7 of this chapter. The quote is from the preface, p. v.*

dollars, he has to become involved in black market currency deals, and in order to "legalize" sales of cars from foreigners to Vietnamese, he must grease the palms of customs officials. When a car he is to sell needs repair, it has to be done with spare parts available only from smugglers. Mr. Nguyen is a dedicated public servant who insists, "I want to do something for my country." But like most government employees, from the $20-a-month secretary up to the underpaid cabinet officer, he feels it necessary to resort to some measure of corrupt and illegal activity in order to make a decent living.[1]

In South Vietnam the ancient Asian tradition flourishes as nowhere else: the tradition that public position, including military leadership, is a road to private gain. General Nguyen Khanh was First Army Corps commander at the time he led 3,000 troops in the overthrow of Diem's successors' regime on January 30, 1964. A *New York Herald Tribune* story about him three days later included this: "As for himself, Gen. Khanh said, he is now in a position to flee South Viet Nam with $10 million and 'live an easy-going life—but I have chosen this.' "[2] He was 37 years old at the time.

Philippe Devillers told me that Madame Ky in conversation with a friend of his said something like this: "You know, we can't be sure how long my husband will be in office, so we have to accumulate all we can in a short time."[3] A CBS news report has told details of the thousands of dollars the Premier receives every week "off the top" from betting at the Saigon racetrack, which in this peculiar war still runs a full schedule of horse racing. Ky admits the money comes to him but claims that it is used "for social welfare activities," particularly among wounded soldiers. He opened the account ledger to CBS correspondent Bill Stout, who found large sums—$5,000 to $15,000—"were frequently paid directly to Ky in cash."[4] A House subcommittee staff member visiting Saigon was told that the track would be an ideal location for painfully needed warehouses, but "we can't touch it" because of the Premier.

Corruption as a way of life is to be found at every level of South Vietnam's society, both military and civilian, according to scores of public and private reports. One of these comes in a letter, entered in the *Congressional Record* by Senator Church, from an American psychological-warfare advisor in whose area the Vietnamese government—with American funds—was paying the salaries of 338 pacification cadres for five villages. But, said his letter, there were only 50 to 60 working there. "So this meant a group of about three minor government officials (Vietnamese) were stealing $4,000 per month." He raised such a fuss over it, presumably with Vietnamese officials, "that they transferred me out to a straight combat unit."[5]

At Bien Hoa, the American Air Force lieutenant colonel in charge of supplies during the rapid buildup of 1966 was desperately in need of more warehouse space. He located materials for a temporary building and put in footings—but the Vietnamese base commander had them torn out. He offered to have his men completely overhaul and inventory the Vietnamese depot if he could use the space they would save—but the Vietnamese officer laughed at his proposal. Forced to double-deck an existing warehouse, he needed some prefabricated structural materials—but his supply was stuck on a waiting ship in Saigon harbor.

So he asked the Vietnamese officer, who had plenty of the needed materials (furnished by the U.S.), to loan him 60 bundles of Dexion until his supply could reach him perhaps a month later. Now the ARVN officer was ready to help out—provided his repayment was 120 bundles, not 60. The American, over a barrel, agreed to the deal, and the 60 extra bundles of versatile and valuable materials sank without a trace in the black market. The Vietnamese officer may never attain General Khanh's $10 million, but obviously he is trying.[6]

"The possibilities for illicit gain," says a House committee report, "through such practices as speculative hoarding, black-marketeering, theft, and smuggling are almost unlimited in an economy operating under the conditions that prevailed in Vietnam earlier this year (1966). As one commentator stated then, 'It appears that running parallel with the war is a national symphony of theft, corruption, and bribery.'"[7]

Theft, corruption, and bribery depend on opportunity. *The U.S. economic aid program costs us more than the Ky government's own entire national budget to run the country.*[8] Our AID personnel in Vietnam, 3,800 strong, numbers more than the entire Washington AID staff of 3,500; in less than 5 years it has had 5 different directors. Out of every $4 spent for U.S. economic assistance throughout the world, $1 goes to Vietnam. The $728,500,000 spent for economic aid to Vietnam in fiscal 1966 is enough to provide nearly $50 each for every man, woman, and child in that country. It is not too far from half the entire Gross National Product, which amounts to $110 per capita.[9]

It should not be surprising, then, that so much of what we ship to Vietnam never reaches the people we say it is intended for. There is theft on the docks, disappearance of truckloads of materials in transport, and further leakage in the provinces; we accomplish part of our purposes only because we pour in such enormous quantities. An official estimate by AID administrator William S. Gaud on January 10, 1967 put our losses at 5 to 6 per cent of all U.S.–financed goods entering Vietnam—"stolen or otherwise 'diverted' before reaching proper recipients. No one knows what percentage reaches Viet Cong hands."[10] The AID figure would indicate a loss of around $25 million in 1966.

The Moss committee report, based on hearings held in the area and official investigation, found losses running far higher. It quotes the then deputy director of AID/Saigon as saying that "at least 60 per cent of the aid is diverted from the purpose for which it is intended."[11] Estimates of pilferage and diversion from the Saigon docks alone ranged from 5 to 40 per cent, and that is only the port of entry into a leaky pipeline. Cement, fertilizer, steel, and other products paid for by American taxpayers reach their destination, if at all, in much shrunken amounts. Vietnamese trucks, both civilian and military, under contract to haul U.S.-paid supplies, cannot be stopped and searched by our military police. In an effort to cut losses, the Saigon port operations security office has assigned hundreds of noncommissioned officers to truck convoy duty, with military police patrols and security guards escorting trucks in groups of three to six to see that they make it from the docks to the warehouses.

One reporter has told of the sort of incident which made such provisions necessary. A shipment for a military post exchange was picked up by seven trucks, but only five arrived at the PX. Two were missing, fully loaded.

"When the PX brass went after the truck contractor," says the account, "he shrugged his shoulders: 'What two trucks?' he said. 'I have only five trucks. Those other two did not belong to me.' They couldn't touch him and another bundle of PX-stamped cigarettes and what-have-you went into circulation 'sopping up loose money.' "[12]

That last phrase alludes to the method we have employed in our efforts to halt inflation. AID's "underlying philosophy," says the Moss report, "was to flood the Vietnamese markets with enough AID commodities to 'sop up' the excess local currency." The result has been the Commercial Import Program (CIP) which the Moss study concluded "was contributing to—rather than preventing—widespread abuses." Under it, AID purchases goods in dollars for Vietnamese importers, who pay for them in piasters. The local currency goes into a joint U.S.–Vietnamese account, providing funds for expenses in Vietnam, including a large share—34 billion piasters out of 75 billion—of the South Vietnam budget.

In addition to providing piasters for "in-country" use, the imports are supposed to drain off piasters from the war-inflated economy where otherwise the shortage of goods would push up prices to ever higher inflationary levels. Our dollars paid to suppliers (we pick up the shipping costs) come back to us only as piasters, so that imports from such non-U.S. sources as Japan, Taiwan, and other countries contribute to the balance-of-payments deficit—officially about $750 million per year but actually considerably more.[13]

The remarkable CIP system has operated on a "free enterprise" or "market demand" basis, providing goods to Vietnamese importers licensed by their own government, not ours. Before reforms spurred by the Moss committee, all of the 2,000 importers in the closed system had received their licenses under the notorious Diem government between 1956 and 1961, when the Nhus controlled much of the country's economic activity. Until devaluation of the piaster in June 1966 the importers paid for their goods at the artificial rate of 60 piasters to the dollar (now 118). With the black market offering 180 to the dollar, the lucky importer in effect received his goods at a third of their value. Importers with CIP licenses have made fortunes in cement, steel, pharmaceuticals, and all kinds of items. One can only speculate how much they have paid corrupt Government of Vietnam officials for their licensing privileges. An individual license for each specific quantity of CIP imports is supposed to be granted free by the Vietnam government, but the Moss committee was told that approval of these licenses involved an "under the table" payment of about 6 piasters for each dollar authorized. This single source of graft could yield GVN officials as much as $15 million at 1966 import levels.

Leaving the Vietnamese government to police the "free enterprise" importers, the Commercial Import Program was, in the House committee's words, "left unmanaged, unaudited and without concern." There was no attempt (although more recently some "commodity analysts" have been employed) to determine how much of any one item would fulfill South Vietnam's legitimate needs. Consequently "the large quantities of such commodities as iron and steel mill products, industrial machinery and parts, cement, pharmaceuticals and chemicals being imported into Vietnam were excessive."[14]

No one knows how much cement from these sources has gone into Viet Cong tunnels. American-made lathes and welding equipment have been found in VC jungle factories. In one discovery of an enemy base camp, reported on June 29, 1966 by CBS News, enough supplies were found "to keep a Vietcong regiment going for four and a half years." Among them were some 6,000 pieces of 3' x 6' corrugated metal; over

1,000 gallons of kerosene—some in sealed cans with U.S. trademarks; 1,500 tons of rice (we supply surplus rice to Vietnam under Food for Peace); and a VC post exchange complete with luxury items.

Because most requests for import of legitimate commodities have gone unquestioned, there have been such incidents as the silver nitrate, sugar, and "unicel" scandals.

Silver nitrate imports, supposedly for silvering mirrors, for photographic use, and for use as an antiseptic, were fifteen times the estimated possible usage in such legitimate ways in 1965. Silver nitrate can be treated to recover both pure silver and nitrate, an ingredient of explosives. With a "pegged" price of 60 piasters for one dollar's worth, treating it—which can be done "in the back of any shack," according to one official—yielded silver worth about 200 piasters. If the silver is hoarded instead of sold, it becomes "an inflation-proof asset which can be sold for hard currency at any time—whether in Saigon or in some other country to which [the owner] has taken his silver in the form of spoons or bullion."[15]

The $10-million "sugar scandal" involved a low grade of sugar bought as first grade from another Asian source by the GVN for its government-owned refinery. There nothing much was done to it except to put it into sacks labeled "Made in Vietnam." From there, instead of going on the market at the official (first grade) price of about 10.5 cents a pound, much of it wound up in the black market at double the price. "A good part of the sugar profits," says U.S. News and World Report, "if reports you hear in Saigon are true, goes into the pockets of some prominent officials of the Vietnamese Government."[16]

Perhaps the most flagrant case of illegal diversion (now stopped) was the importation of a chemical known as "unicel." A 50-ton shipment, supposedly for use in making rubber-soled tennis shoes, aroused the curiosity of a State Department inspector general who was intrigued by the apparent huge demand for sneakers and by the chemical name (dinitrosopentamethaline tetramine). Tests by the Naval Ordnance laboratory revealed explosive properties almost as great as TNT. But 100 tons were shipped from the U.S., as well as quantities from Japan and Taiwan, before importation of the lethal product was halted. A single pound of the stuff, packed with a fuse into a bicycle hand-pump—a method used by Saigon terrorists—"could wreck a building," officials said.[17]

There are many other ways in which the CIP operation, virtually uncontrolled by our AID program except for the doling out of funds, has been a prolific source of corruption and of supplies for the Viet Cong.

Shipments show up with less than the manifest calls for: the Liberian ship *Kimon*, for example, had 878 bags of rice "lost" by the time her cargo reached the warehouse, while there were another 669 empty bags and nearly 6,000 bags of wet, unsalable rice.[18] 84,000 Nicholson files imported under the CIP showed up in Bangkok, to which they had been re-exported and sold on the open market; since twenty Saigon firms had imported Nicholson files, there was no way of pinning down the Vietnamese culprit. Rice from Thailand has been overpriced on shipping charges by 100 per cent—and the companies involved were "suspected Chinese Communist agents."[19]

Falsification of the country of origin has resulted in cement delivered from "another Asian country" whose outside "free world" wrapper covered a wrapper showing that it had actually been manufactured in North Vietnam—and inside the inner wrapper there was even Communist propaganda literature![20] Goods are hoarded illegally in order to bring more as inflation pushes prices up. A Chinese businessman in Saigon "openly admitted" to a reporter that his two warehouses were full of imported cement; he was holding out for 325 piasters per bag, nearly triple the government control rate.[21]

"PX Alley" is notorious as the street in Saigon where you can buy anything available in our post exchanges—sometimes even before an item has reached the shelves there—from cigarettes and beer to hairspray, army shirts, and transistor radios, often at prices about three times the PX price. Nor are Vietnamese the only ones susceptible to the disease of corruption; in the fall of 1966 there were at least 400 Americans, both military and civilian, facing official action for black market or currency offenses of various kinds. An American officer with a $10,000 income was caught after sending home $20,000 in money orders. In the notorious hairspray affair, an inventory showed 67,000 cans—a sixteen-year supply for the 700 women eligible to buy it—in the Saigon-Cholon PX; it is both a good black-market item and a favorite form of payment to prostitutes. The PX manager was eventually fired and much of the hairspray sent to Guam and Okinawa.[22] In December 1966 a reporter writing from Danang revealed that the post exchange there was currently "short 400,000 cases of beer."[23]

In March 1966 a Chinese businessman of Saigon, convicted of profiteering by overpricing cloth, giving a 150,000-piaster bribe, and illegal speculation, was executed by a firing squad. The sudden crackdown, singling out 34-year-old millionaire Ta Vinh, who left three wives and eight children, was greeted in Saigon as "hypocritical, harsh and over-hasty." The general reaction was, wrote a Scripps-Howard reporter, "So he was corrupt? Isn't everybody?" Said the *Saigon Daily News:* "Myriads of lice and leeches, officials and non-officials—it is their corruptness that makes possible the existence of Ta Vinhs."[24]

The truth is that as we have poured millions upon millions of dollars into the "third war" in Vietnam we have done incalculable moral as well as economic damage to that society. We have not only tried to satiate the voracious appetites of war, but we have fed the "lice and leeches" while they spawn and multiply, weakening the whole fabric of an already weak social structure. Money, like power, tends to corrupt, and our money has gone far to spread corruption: so far, indeed, that we have succeeded in undermining the very principles of self-reliant democracy. For we have tried to substitute our money for their lack of dedication and lack of leadership.

Look at what happened in Rachkien, a Delta village 20 miles from Saigon. Into this "thoroughly Vietcong-dominated area," as we have begun to do increasingly where the locals are unenthusiastic and uncooperative, we sent a battalion "to rid the area of Communists." The commander, Lieutenant Colonel Charles Gillis, found the streets very dirty. He asked the American AID man why the people didn't get together and clean them up.

" 'We asked them about that,' the AID man said, 'and they told us they would do it if we would pay them to do it.'

" 'Pay them to clean their own streets?' Gillis asked.

" 'Yes, sir,' the AID man said.

" 'Pay them to clean their own streets,' Gillis repeated again, shaking his head.

" 'It's Vietnam, sir,' someone else said."[25]

It is difficult for us, not being Vietnamese, to conceive of the vast scale—in relation to their economy—on which we pour money into their country. We see a billion dollars as less than one per cent of our national budget, or as little more than a tenth of one per cent of a Gross National Product now at a rate of over $800 billion in a year. But let us try to translate our money into terms of South Vietnam's economy.

Our economic aid in fiscal 1966 totaled $727.5 million, as I have noted. The Military Assistance Command in January 1966 estimated that each of our troops spends $45 per month in piasters; at 390,000 men that comes to $540 each for a year, or $210 million. Military contractors and their employees spend 8.25 billion piasters or $70 million more for a total of more than $1 billion.[26]

At the World Bank figure of $110 per capita, the South Vietnamese GNP for 15,730,000 people totals $1,730,000,000, so that our

$1,007,500,000 is an additional 67 per cent dropped into that small economy. With America's GNP at $730 billion, 67 per cent would be a staggering $489 billion! It is only fair to note, however, that perhaps as much as a quarter of the total input is in the form of goods which do not involve payment in piasters.

But what kind of economic chaos would strike our economy if we added even $350 billion to it in a year? Says the Moss report: "The tremendous infusion of piasters into Vietnam's economy . . . has brought about a classic inflationary situation with too much money chasing too few goods. Much of the need for additional piasters has been met simply by printing additional quantities of banknotes as needed." So great was the inflationary pressure that the cost of living in Vietnam rose in the second quarter of 1966 at an annual rate of 74 per cent.[27]

Such a drastic squeeze on purchasing power is a tremendous incentive for individuals, especially those living on fixed incomes, to find (as did Mr. Nguyen) some means of adding to fast-diminishing buying power. What we have done to the economy by inducing such great inflation is to increase "moonlighting," black-marketing, currency manipulation, theft, speculation, and all the other forms of corruption. To a considerable degree we have not only expanded the opportunities, but in many cases we have created the necessity for such actions if people are to exist. In the military, galloping inflation without corresponding pay increases creates severe morale problems. At the same time, raises can only feed the inflationary spiral.

Let me make one more comparison, this time on a more personal basis. Mr. Nguyen's U.S. opposite number as third-high man in his government department would probably receive at least 20 times Mr. Nguyen's $100 a month, while the average U.S. secretary's modest pay, say $400 a month, would likewise be at least 20 times that of her $20-a-month Saigon sister. By these standards, the little secretary transplanted to our midst from a fabulously affluent society would have $96,000 a year from her job, while the bureaucrat would earn an annual $480,000. A very ordinary $7,200-a-year American as compared to a Vietnamese average citizen with—let us be generous—$50 a month has an income equivalent to $86,400. Is it any wonder that in poor countries every American is looked upon as rich?

February 9, 1967 was the beginning of the Year of the Goat, celebrated with the gift-giving and festivities of *Tet*, the lunar new year holiday. The price of gifts (most often clothes) reflected the hardships of inflation. "It's terrible," a reporter quoted a young secretary. "Last year it cost me 500 piasters (about $4) for a new pair of shoes for my baby brother. This year it was a thousand. And the *ao dais!** It used to be 200, now they want 300 or 500, or 600." Still, not all Vietnamese feel the pinch—there are many among whom the status symbol is a chauffeur-driven Mercedes sedan.[28]

There can be no question that AID is now making efforts to tighten up the long-ailing Commercial Import Program, to expand the educational, medical, and agricultural work of its technical-assistance program, and to carry out its assignments more effectively. The CIP is no longer, thanks largely to the Moss committee, left wide open to corruption without checks: a January 1967 AID report details a series of reforms, and in a solid factual manner without the flamboyant "we're doing great" style of other reports.[29] There are dedicated people in AID in Vietnam, but the economic war is as difficult, and as unpromising in many respects, as the military and political wars.

Although in the past I have supported our foreign aid program, in 1966 and again in 1967 I voted against it. We are spending large sums for objectives we are not achieving, and nowhere more than in Vietnam. The United Nations is equipped through the Food and Agriculture Organization, World Health Organization, and a host of technical-assistance and economic programs, to respond to world aid needs in a way superior to any unilateral effort we can make—partly because as Americans our understanding of Asians and Africans is so limited. We should be channeling our resources through these instruments instead of relying on an effort—splendidly conceived and greatly useful in the Marshall Plan days before such U.N. development as we now have —which time and changing circumstance have outmoded.

Our Vietnam economic aid (and much of our other foreign aid, for that matter) is not given in the dominantly unselfish spirit which animates United Nations agencies with their more disinterested concern for the less developed countries. Rather, as an adjunct of the war effort it places our needs and purposes, our plans and desires, above those of the ordinary Vietnamese. By working closely with a government which evidences far more concern for the wealthy, the landowners, and the military-political leadership than for the people themselves, we prevent our assistance from reaching those for whom it was intended.

Supporters of the administration counter these arguments by pointing out that a certain amount of the corruption and waste in our aid in South Vietnam is inevitable and avoidable. But this rebuttal does not answer the central points made in this chapter—namely that the eco-

---

* The ao dai, *the traditional national dress of Vietnamese women, is particularly used at* Tet *instead of Western dress.*

nomic war, like the military and the political wars, is not successfully or effectively accomplishing the goals of the United States.[30]

Our aid effort, like the total policy of which it is a part, does not represent the best that the American people have to offer to the Vietnamese people. Neither is it an effective use of our resources. Unfortunately, it is probably the case that the American aid program is doing more harm than good in South Vietnam. This could be true because of the corruption that is being fostered and sustained among the governing classes upon the American aid largess. This aid is enriching an already exceedingly advantaged urban class in an underdeveloped agrarian nation.

In sum, the sad fact is that we are not building anything permanent, good or useful for the Vietnamese people by our aid expenditures. Moreover, these expenditures are greatly out of line with the reasonable and proper priorities that should be established so that our limited resources can meet the demands being made by all of the developing countries of the world.

Given the circumstances, that is perhaps inevitable. But the fact remains that the third war, the economic war, like the military and the political wars, is far from a success. Perhaps some day, working through the international agencies, we can genuinely improve the economic life of Vietnam in a peacetime war against poverty, disease, and illiteracy, in clear perspective with the claims of all other needy areas as well. But the first task is to settle the military conflict, whose cost to the Vietnamese far outweighs the effects, so often deleterious, of our efforts on the economic front.

IX

Counting the Costs

A report released by the Pentagon stated that through August 1967 a total of 15,154 American servicemen had died in Vietnam. 12,605 had been killed in battle and 2,549 deaths had occurred from other causes.

Along with these American men killed, another 77,153 had been wounded in action and there were an additional 161,250 casualties from other causes.[1]

It is not really possible for anyone who has not been directly affected to comprehend the significance of these casualties. The use of numbers and quantitative categories is a poor substitute for an understanding of human beings. Because the Vietnam war continues, tens of thousands of young Americans and Vietnamese will never be able to live out their lives. And how can one describe the pain, the suffering, the sense of untimely death felt by all of those people who have suffered but yet must go on living?

This is a brutal war. The soldier in the field often feels that he is enmeshed in a personal struggle for survival rather than viewing the fighting in terms of the often repeated cliches used by those on the home front.[2] As in all wars, those who must experience it and live through it often incur mental reactions which are more painful than physical wounds. A society that is geared to war and killing is not a society that nurtures compassion and understanding for all of the other people on this earth with whom we must live. Its cost is high in many ways, only one of which is financial.

Marines from the Seventh Fleet task force slogged through the mangrove swamps and rice paddies of Kien Hoa, 35 miles south of Saigon, in January 1967 after an amphibious assault landing for Operation Deckhouse V. After nine days of an intense sweep against what was supposed to be a Viet Cong training and supply-base area with a rest and recreation center, the Marines turned back to their floating base. If earlier there had been a concentration there of VC troops from among the 80,000 in the Delta, advance intelligence of the push—even bar girls in Saigon knew about it a week in advance—had allowed them to slip away.

The drive was supposed to cut across Kien Hoa, an island province with confluent rivers separating it from its neighbors, and push perhaps thousands of Viet Cong to the sea. It netted just 21 enemy dead and 14 captured. One of the most expensive single offensives of the war, the operation included assault boats patroling the rivers, two battalions of Vietnamese marines and other troops put in place by boat and helicopter, and ships stationed in the South China Sea to seal off that escape route. At an estimated $16 million spent—nearly $2 million a day—the cost per Viet Cong killed in this one drive was some $800,000.[3] There were then at least a million and a half civilian refugees in dire need, whose government allowance (for those who receive it) is about $10 per person per year. The cost of Operation Deckhouse V alone was enough to pay that entire bill.

There are two kinds of casualty figures reported—those of enemy losses and those of our own dead and wounded. As to the first, the Viet Cong "body count," skepticism is widespread and apparently well founded. It is natural to want to put the best possible face on the war, and one way to do it is to estimate enemy losses at as high a figure as possible and to put our own as low as we can. "Nothing is phonier," writes Arthur Schlesinger, Jr., "than the spurious exactitude of our statistics about the Vietnam war. . . . The 'body count' of dead Vietcong, for example, includes heaven knows how many innocent bystanders and could hardly be more unreliable."[4]

Before the big buildup of 1964–65 an American "advisor" wrote in a letter to a friend: "They said my battalion (250 men) killed or captured 175 Vietcong. However, I have seen only two bodies and about eight prisoners in all our actions. Even accounting for the ones dragged away after they're dead by the Vietcong, I think we killed only 20."[5]

Donald Duncan, ten-year Army veteran and the first enlisted man in Vietnam to be nominated for the Legion of Merit, has detailed his experience as a Master Sergeant under 28 hours of close-support bombing against an estimated 300 Viet Cong at a plantation headquarters. His comment is enlightening as to both casualty estimates and the effectiveness of our bombing. "When I came out," he says, "it was estimated they had killed about 250 Vietcong in the first day. They asked me how many Vietcong did I think they had killed and I said maybe six, and I was giving them the benefit of the doubt at that. The bombing had no real military significance. It would only work if aimed at concentrated targets such as villages."[6]

The estimated number of Viet Cong killed, in fact, runs about as high as the estimated number of regular enemy troops infiltrating from the North—four to five times U.S.–South Vietnam losses combined—and yet our estimate of the total number of enemy forces in the South keeps growing. Either they are still gaining recruits in South Vietnam despite our claims that they have exhausted Southern manpower, or there is something wrong with our figures.

No modern war can be justified in economic terms any more than in terms of human lives. But there can be no doubt that the economic costs of military operations in Vietnam have soared to heights far beyond any previous experience, as we pour in vast quantities of bombs, rockets, ammunition, planes, and sophisticated hardware of all kinds—more than any previous war has consumed, and all transported expensively halfway around the world.

The area of North and South Vietnam combined is a little more than that of New York State, while the population—with only half a dozen cities of more than 100,000—is about double that state's. When you consider the expanse of jungle, the density of the rural population becomes even more striking. Into this area in 1966 we poured 637,000 tons of bombs—just a little less than the 656,000 tons we dropped on the entire Pacific theater during all of World War II. *That is more than 5 tons for every square mile, one ton for every 51 people.* We who have never known a bomb on our own land can scarcely comprehend such figures.[7]

A single B-52 flying from Guam—a 10-hour trip at $1,300 per hour of flying time—can carry eighty-four 500-pound and twenty-four 750-pound bombs for a total load of more than 29 tons. With an average of

425 B-52 sorties per month at $13,000 each for flight cost and $60,000 for bombs (bombs average about $1 per pound), some $30 million was spent in 1966 solely for active operation costs of these big planes.[8] An F-4 aircraft costs $2,500,000; an F-100, $800,000. The average cost of a fixed-wing aircraft is $1.8 million, and since, by our own figures, average losses are running to more than 10 a week, we are losing a total of $900,000,000 worth of aircraft a year.

Although we have 510 supply ships in the 11,000-mile U.S.–Vietnam run, we are flying more men and weapons to combat by cargo planes than in any previous war—900 flights a month, with their attendant high cost. The flow of supplies is 600,000 tons a month and rising.

Ground troops spray jungle shadows with bullets from their M-14 rifles at a rate up to 150 rounds per minute. With an M-16, ammunition consumption in one minute is as great as 750 men could supply with single-shot rifles in the Civil War. From an A-47 plane or a helicopter up to 18,000 rounds per minute stream from air to ground in the hope that a few may hit an elusive target. As long ago as January 1966, Secretary McNamara testified that ground forces were using ammunition "at the rate of about $100 million per month," a rate which had increased to $120 million by December. During the same period the expenditure of air munitions jumped even more, from $110 million per month in January to $142 million per month in December.[9] Artillery shells are expensive; Bernard Fall wrote from "Artillery Plateau" of "unobserved H-and-I [harassment and interdiction] fire on targets deeply shrouded in fog, at $168 a shell."[10] The purpose of such random fire into the jungle is merely to keep the Viet Cong at bay. It is little wonder—or perhaps rather it is something to be wondered at—that artillery ammunition is being spent in little South Vietnam in quantities greater than those used by U.S. forces in World War II.[11]

In the last 20 years, the development of rockets and missiles—42 different missile systems from Atlas to Hound Dog to Walleye are listed in the index to the Senate procurement authorization hearings for fiscal 1967—have raised the costs to further exorbitant heights. The Shrike, for example, is a special-purpose missile designed to home in on radar installations. One costs $14,000, and the fiscal 1967 procurement plan scheduled 1,800 of them at a cost of more than $25 million. But with scores of radar installations in North Vietnam, they have a record of frequently aiming at one, only to become "beguiled by another and wind up doing nothing."[12] The result is that the Shrike, as Hanson W. Baldwin reports, "has destroyed only a few of its targets."[13]

Plane production, with 800 to 1,000 bombers and fighter-bombers scheduled for fiscal 1967, was in September 1966 ordered increased by 280 for the year beginning July 1, 1967.[14] But in December the rate of production had not yet caught up with the "attrition rate" (combat losses plus other losses). The new budget and the supplemental request of January 1967 provided for procurement of 2,542 planes and 2,451 helicopters.

The escalation of costs continues to climb. Instead of going to the "front" in $1,300 jeeps and $15,000 six-by-six trucks, as in World War II, troops go to battle in $250,000 helicopters, which are highly accident-prone as well as subject to being shot down. Of 177 helicopters lost in 1965 only 76 fell to "hostile action"; the other 101 were lost in accidental crashes and other mishaps.[15] The Cessna O-1 observation plane used as a spotter in South Vietnam costs $24,000; it is being replaced by the North American OV-10 at $325,000. The Douglas A-1 Skyraider at $85,000 is being phased out in favor of the A-7 Corsair with a price tag above $1 million.[16]

It is no wonder, then, that the direct cost of this "little" war in Vietnam has mounted to at least $2.5 billion per month, and more probably $2.7 billion, or some $30 billion a year, with every sign of further increases.[17] The defense budget for fiscal 1967 asked new spending authorizations of $75.3 billion—only $5.7 billion less than the amount spent during the peak World War II year of 1945.° The Defense Department's anticipated spending in fiscal 1968 is greater than the total *national* budgets (not just defense) of Great Britain, France, and West Germany combined. Although the administration denies any intention to seek an additional supplemental appropriation "barring unforeseen developments in Vietnam or elsewhere in the world," rigid planning eighteen to thirty months in advance is obviously impossible. (The 1967 supplemental request was for $12.9 billion.)[18]

We have been told repeatedly that we can bear the costs of Vietnam without much more than inconvenience to the economy. Yet $30 billion for Vietnam equals three-quarters of the entire federal budget for 1950, when we spent $39.6 billion for all purposes, including the defense establishment. The cost of Vietnam at $30 billion is almost 20 per cent of the current $135 billion total administrative budget. To tell the American people that the costs of this war are insignificant is to be untruthful. For the American people to believe they are insignificant is to be unrealistic.

How much is $30 billion?

It is nearly $40 million per day for 365 days in the year. It is nearly

° *Though that sum was much greater, of course, in terms of constant dollars.*

$3,500,000 per hour twenty-four hours per day; $56,844 per minute; $947 every single second of the year.

$30 billion is more than double the U.S. gold reserves.

With $30 billion you could have bought in 1966 all the clothes and accessories sold by every men's store in the country, plus everything sold by the nation's women's apparel and accessory stores in the entire year. You could then add all the shoes sold by every retail shoe store in the country; buy up everything sold by every retail drugstore for the year; and drain the nation's liquor stores of everything they sold during the year. You would then be down to $600 million of pocket money.[19]

With $30 billion you could give more than $150 to every man, woman and child in this country—or a color television set to every family. Or you could make the South Vietnamese truly wealthy with $2,000 for every one of them down to the last peasant farmer—$10,000 for a family of five. Conversely, of course, to pay for $30 billion poured into the Vietnam war will cost $150 for every man, woman and child in the United States.

The effect of Vietnam at home is not entirely obvious, since much of the impact is hidden in a slowdown of our rate of economic advance rather than in actual cutbacks of a stringent and sharply felt nature. It is true that we can have both "guns and butter" in our rich economy. But what is spent for one cannot be spent for the other, and when there is less butter we can only spread it thinner. That truth has become strikingly obvious in the 90th Congress.

For thousands of Americans our growing casualties *are* the war—its economic cost is secondary. This is as it should be. The losses and suffering which have been inflicted on Americans serving in this war should never be minimized. But the effect of the fighting on individuals is only a portion of the total cost of the war. Certainly that cost cannot be reckoned without counting also the price which the war has exacted from progress toward both the domestic and the foreign goals of America.

As long as the war in Vietnam continues, our society will be unable to undertake the massive task of eradicating the shortcomings of American society and of improving the quality of American life.

As long as the war in Vietnam continues, the probability is increased that escalation will lead to a wider war, perhaps even World War III; the international atmosphere engendered by Vietnam will preclude the opportunity to work for meaningful detente and to implement "the international rule of law" to which the administration constantly refers.

From 1929 until the early 1950's Americans were preoccupied with a succession of major crises: the depression, World War II, the rise of the cold war, the Korean War, the McCarthy controversy. The remainder of the 1950's was a time of complacency, a turning away from these disagreeable involvements of the recent past, a time of pause and a time of concern with narrower personal affairs.

But in the 1960's we began to perceive that a whole range of domestic problems required urgent attention. The period of complacency was ending as our society began to look at itself more critically. The American people agreed that there was much to be done to improve the conditions of American life, to bring its realities closer to its potentials.

In other words, there were many problems which had been brought about by the changing patterns of life in the mid-20th century. Previously, our energies had been involved elsewhere and were not available to be channeled to meet these problems. The period 1960–1965 was distinguished by the growing awareness of the importance and magnitude of these problems. Also, there was a growing agreement, until 1965, that our society should attempt to resolve these problems.

This movement reached its peak in the election of 1964 and carried into 1965. Here was the clear and ringing commitment to repair the malfunctions in American society. Here was the sanction by the voters that the basis for American leadership was the sterling example of the quality of American life. Here was the promise that we should not and could not send American boys to do the job that Asian boys should be doing.

The decision to escalate the war in Vietnam, to substitute American military power for the political failures of Diem and his successors, killed the movement summarized above just as dead as a body in the field in Vietnam. This was a cost of the Vietnam war.

The energies devoted to fighting this war, the divisive splits among Americans, the promises broken, these are costs of the Vietnam war. These conditions categorically preclude the patient and expensive task of improving the domestic environment.

The riots during the summer of 1967 were merely the most striking and frightening symptom of the failure to meet the pressing domestic needs. The dilemmas of both urban and farm societies do not riot. Higher taxes do not riot. Air pollution and water pollution do not riot. The critical shortages in social, educational, and health services do not riot. If they did, perhaps more people would come to realize the mounting domestic costs of the war in Vietnam.

We have been told again and again by the administration that the

United States is rich enough to pay for both Vietnam and domestic improvements. However appealing this may be as a theory, the realities demonstrate that such an idea is pure nonsense.

Most people who examine the past and the facts will comprehend that American society will not undertake two efforts of such magnitude simultaneously. Walter Lippmann put this idea succinctly when he wrote that advocating the sentiment that our society "can have two overwhelming preoccupations at the same time is the mark of an amateur."

It is a paradox and a tragedy that skilled and talented leadership has come to rightfully deserve being judged as "amateur." This is a cost of the Vietnam war.

In 1966 the federal budget, facing the financing problems of our growing Vietnam buildup, recommended several ways of spreading the butter thinner. All were at the expense of the projected improvement of the quality of American life. One proposal was to cut the school lunch program by $19 million. Another was to slash the school milk program by 80 per cent from $103 million to $21 million, an $82 million "saving" which would have paid for two days of the war at the expense of needy children. A cut of $175 million from National Defense Education Act loan funds was another recommendation. In all three cases Congress refused to go along with the recommendations.

The budget proposals of 1967 likewise contained some cutbacks, mostly effected by calling for appropriations at a lower level than the sums already authorized for various programs. Recommendations included a stretch-out in authorized highway spending; limitation of new public works projects—such as dams and reservoirs—to a very small number, with reduced funding for others; a cutback in new funds for building health research and college facilities; holding to a minimum increased aid for elementary and secondary education; less than half the authorized funds for aiding cities and states with water-pollution programs; a drop of $6 million from the previous year in funds for aiding cities with their mass-transit problems; a request for $40 million in the rent subsidy program where $70 million had been authorized; a sharp cut in funds for the Food-for-Peace program—designed to stimulate self-help by the recipient countries—from the $3 billion authorized to only $1.8 billion in the new budget. The healthy increase for Social Security, financed by separate taxes through a separate trust fund, could be recommended without affecting the $135 billion administrative budget. In 1968 the Congressional clamor for more cuts, as well as the administration's plea for a surtax, is even louder.

Since our population continues to grow—we have added more than

20 million people since the 1960 census to reach the 200,000,000 mark —whenever we fail to advance we do not simply stand still, we fall behind. In spite of Vietnam, the total spent for "Great Society" programs in fiscal 1967 (July 1, 1966 to June 30, 1967) was $4.8 billion above the previous year, but the increase called for in the budget submitted in early 1967 was only $1.9 billion.[20] A cut of such magnitude in the rate of increase is a measure of how thin domestic "butter" is being spread. Measured against the increase in Gross National Product it is a 50 per cent decrease, from 8 per cent of 1966 GNP's gain ($59.6 billion) to 4.5 per cent of the 1967 GNP increase ($41.7 billion).[21]

In addition to the constriction of hopeful programs already under way, there are new and promising legislative proposals whose consideration will languish while Vietnam continues to draw so heavily upon federal resources. Two of these whose chances are dimmed by the war are the federal-state tax-sharing proposal and the "negative income tax" or guaranteed annual income, both of which have drawn support from conservation economists as well as liberals; the argument will be, "We need all the federal income right now . . . wait."

The myth that war actually helps the civilian economy is blasted by the recent careful study of Columbia University Professor Emile Benoit and Dr. Harold Lubell of the Agency for International Development (AID), working under a Ford Foundation grant. They analyzed the fiscal 1965 defense budget of $51.4 billion in careful detail to see how much of it went for purposes that actually aided the civilian economy. They found that $46.1 billion, or about 90 per cent, "represented resources that had to be taken from other uses that might have increased the material well-being of the American people."[22]

Another economic cost of the war in Vietnam is the damage it does to our international balance of payments position. In 1963 our balance of payments deficit—a situation in which more dollars leave the country than return to it—was $2.7 billion; and in 1964, $2.8 billion. The Treasury inaugurated a series of strenuous efforts to cut the deficit—such as encouraging American firms to borrow abroad for their foreign capital needs and discouraging foreign travel by U.S. citizens. Thanks in large part to the voluntary cooperation of business, it was possible to cut the deficit for 1965 to $1.4 billion. But as we began to spend more and more dollars in Vietnam the outflow once more increased the dollar drain. In May 1966, Secretary of the Treasury Henry H. Fowler estimated that "the direct and indirect costs of Viet Nam will increase the U.S.'s deficit by at least $1.4 billion this year." According to *Time* magazine, "Unaccounted hoards of U.S. dollars flow from banks in Viet Nam [where banking is mainly in French hands] to the Banque de France, which promptly turns them in for U.S. gold."[23] The French drain on our gold has been widely reported and is a most disturbing phenomenon. U.S. gold reserves by May 1966—the date of Fowler's statement—had reached a 28-year low of $13.7 billion. They have since dropped still further, to $12.9 billion following devaluation of the pound in November 1967.

Because of our inability to curb the dollar drain, Vietnam can also take credit for stalling much-needed world monetary reform. The American dollar remains, as it has been for many years, the chief currency for world trade. Dollars can be converted freely into every kind of local money from the Swiss franc to the Japanese yen, the Indian rupee, or the Ghanaian cedi. If dollars are to continue to serve as a world currency, more of them will be needed abroad; and so long as our unfavorable payments balance pumps them out to the world they will be available. But if we succeed in gaining "equilibrium," which would halt the gold drain, there will be a pinch in the world markets as the dollar supply shrinks or fails to grow with international trade. If something else could replace dollars as the medium of international exchange, it would benefit our balance of payments position. Therefore we have tried to spur development of some new unit universally acceptable as the dollar is for international use.

But a new world currency such as the proposed "cru" (currency reserve unit) would probably require drawing on the reserves of participating nations who now let our gold supply back their international (dollar) money medium. Consequently there is no enthusiasm among many members of the International Monetary Fund or the dominant "Group of Ten" for world currency reform until it is forced by lack of dollars in world circulation. Dollars are a preferred medium because their value has not fluctuated as has that of many other currencies; even the pound sterling has been less reliable. The system works, so why disturb it in favor of some untried "paper gold" scheme?

Yet the measure of need for some such world monetary reform is shown by the net decline of the gold supply which backs our dollars. From more than $22.7 billion in 1957 the Treasury's gold reserve has steadily declined year after year to the present level below $13 billion. At the same time foreign gold reserves are also shrinking, largely because some billion dollars' worth of gold disappears annually into the caches of hoarders. In 1966, although gold production hit a record $1.47 billion, for the first time none was added to the world's monetary gold stocks. The U.S. output of $65 million all went for commercial uses. The danger, very simply, is that the load the dollar is forced to carry may some day grow too heavy and result in a loss of stability, a stability to which the fixed Treasury gold purchase price of $35 an ounce across the years has contributed so immeasurably. If that happened there could ensue a worldwide depression and economic chaos unimaginably awesome in its dimensions. We could feel much easier if the world's financial welfare were not tied to the dollar, with all the world's economic health thereby made our own responsibility. But the need for change will not be felt so sharply as to bring about monetary reform while Vietnam aggravates the dollar outflow and prevents achievement of balance in the payments ledger. The "paper gold" proposal, as a *Washington Post* headline put it, is therefore very likely a "war casualty" of Vietnam.[24]

I stated above that a second major cost of the Vietnam war lies in the fact that an escalating war can escalate into World War III. Even if the war were to end, there would not be any returns in increased peace and security for the United States. The basic reason for this is that, as was stated in the campaign in 1964, we cannot bring about progress in all of the evolving countries around the world. Only their native citizens can master that task.

In 1917, President Wilson led this country into a crusade to "make the world safe for democracy," into a war which would "end all wars." No war has ever brought permanent peace. No war can bring permanent peace. War is an excellent device for destroying something, but not for building.

The advancement of peace is precisely the effort of building. It is slow and arduous, but peace must be the basis of the relationship between the major powers in our nuclear age.

There is no panacea, no one victory which can bring peace. The great crusade of 1917, the battle at Armageddon, did not bring world peace. Even the most favorable outcome to the war in Vietnam does not have the prospect of enhancing peace and security for the United States.

To attain peace is to engage in the long and winding process of building trust. Only in an atmosphere of trust will nations be willing to move away from a strict interpretation of national rights and concentrate on neutralizing the threatening and divisive issues. This will not be an easy process. It cannot take place in an atmosphere in which one's rivals are employing massive force according to their own designs.

Why would the most favorable end to the Vietnam war fail to advance the long-term peace and security of the United States? Secretary McNamara has provided a good explanation for this. I think that

McNamara's analysis validates the contention that Vietnam is a vast diversion of American resources which leaves the root problems of discontent and violence untouched.

The Secretary noted that "there is a direct and constant relationship between violence and the economic status of the countries afflicted." Of the 27 rich nations, only one had suffered a major internal uprising. Of the 38 very poor nations, 32 had suffered outbreaks during the same period. Because there is a causal link between low economic status and the outbreak of violence, the Secretary continued that "it would be a gross oversimplification to regard Communism as the central factor in every conflict throughout the underdeveloped world." Given these conditions, it was obvious to McNamara that "without development, there can be no security." Furthermore, it is clear that "the local people themselves are best able to deal directly with the situation in the framework of their own traditions." America can and should help these economically developing nations, but McNamara stated authoritatively that "certainly we have no charter to rescue floundering regimes who have brought violence on themselves by deliberately refusing to meet the legitimate expectations of their citizenry."[25]

The only way in which the last statement does not qualify as an accurate description of the Diem regime is that not only did Diem not meet the legitimate demands of the people but he suppressed them and increased their hardships.

The loss of the opportunity to try to build trust and peace among nations in our nuclear world is a cost of the Vietnam war. The failure to deal with the root causes of discontent and violence in the world is a cost of the Vietnam war.

Finally, the tally of American losses in the continuing war in Vietnam must reckon the intangible cost to our world leadership through erosion of confidence and fading respect of other nations. Many have parted company with us over Vietnam, but for the most part our focus on Vietnam itself has been so intense that we have not noticed our international loss of position. We are no longer cutting off the rest of the world, but now the rest of the world is cutting us off.

We stand all but alone in Vietnam, even though we have formal alliances with 42 nations. There are just four countries supporting us with troops of any kind: Australia, New Zealand, the Philippines, and South Korea. New Zealand's contribution is 150 men. Australia's until the middle of 1966 was 1,400, when it was increased—over considerable opposition—to 4,500. At the time, an Australian paper put the facts bluntly: "We are not increasing our forces to 4,500 in the middle of this year because we have been asked by the present South Vietnamese Government. We are doing it because the Americans want us to and need our moral support . . . because we value America's friendship."[26]

The 2,000 Philippine troops supplied following the U.S. visit of President Ferdinand Marcos in September 1966 are engineers, not fighting men. They are there, as Senator Wayne Morse said in the Senate, "to serve the appearance of support for the war by an Asian country, an appearance the United States desperately needs."[27] Furthermore, President Marcos exacted a price for them in an increase of our foreign aid to the Philippines (to which we have given $1 billion in economic aid since World War II) by $55 million, up from some $20 million previously scheduled for fiscal 1967. In effect the Philippine forces are mercenaries, since in addition to the price in aid exacted from us, we are paying their salaries and their upkeep, and providing their equipment.

The same is true, but on an even larger scale, of the Korean troops in South Vietnam. Korean steel, cement, and other products purchased for our use in Vietnam amounted to $15 million in 1965 and increased considerably in 1966. At the start of that year, when Vice President Humphrey stopped in Korea on his nine-nation Asian tour, the Korean cabinet decided to double its troop contingent—then consisting mainly of its "Fighting Tiger" division—to some 40,000. "In return," *U.S. News and World Report* noted, "Seoul got from the U.S. $150 million in development funds, increased military aid, and an opportunity to sell more goods to the U.S. and South Vietnam. The entire South Korean army [of more than 600,000] is partly paid for and maintained by the U.S."[28] According to the London *Economist*, "South Korean lorry drivers, welders, electricians and assorted technicians, who would earn less than $70 a month in Korea, have been hired by American contractors in Vietnam at salaries ranging from $270 to $450 a month."[29] Its story, captioned "Fighting Tiger for Rent," concluded, "Seoul is likely to offer a few thousand extra fighting tigers in order to get the largest possible share" of economic benefits.

The attitude I found at the highest levels in Japan, India and Pakistan in late 1965 seemed to be quite simply that Vietnam is our war, not theirs.[30] Yet a State Department release says, "At present, 39 nations besides the United States are providing, or have agreed to provide, economic, humanitarian or military aid to the Vietnamese."[31] What is that aid?

Britain, a member of SEATO, gives official lip service to support for the United States in Vietnam. But her contribution at the time of the State Department claim was 11 police instructors, a professor of English, and some technical and construction equipment.[32] A poll by the Gallup organization reported, in November 1966, that 42 per cent of the British people thought we should begin to withdraw our troops from Vietnam, while only 16 per cent favored increasing our attacks on North Vietnam and 17 per cent preferred maintaining the present level of fighting.[33]

France, another SEATO nation, in spite of General De Gaulle's urgings for us to get out, has sent to its former colony 600 educators, medical and technical personnel. The Gallup poll showed a 68 per cent majority of the French—for whom Algeria as well as Vietnam is a recent memory—were for withdrawal of our troops; 8 per cent were for the present level; 5 per cent for an increase. More surprising, and a shocking revelation of the deteriorated American image, was the result of a 1965 French Institute of Public Opinion poll on this question: "In your opinion which chiefs of state constitute the greatest menace for peace?" Mao Tse-tung led the list with 32 per cent of the votes—but close behind him came Lyndon B. Johnson with 30 per cent. Premier Kosygin drew only half as many, 15 per cent.[34]

West Germany, where so many thousands of our troops are stationed, furnished 30 ambulances, 23 technical and medical people, radio batteries, and $20 million in credits. The Gallup poll found 51 per cent of West Germans in favor of our troop withdrawal, 19 per cent for the present level of fighting, 15 per cent for increasing our attacks on the North.[35]

The Japanese newspaper *Asahi Shimbun* conducted its own nation-wide survey of public opinion in Japan in August 1965. 79 per cent of those polled had read or heard of our bombings in North Vietnam; 4 per cent said they supported these bombings, 75 per cent said they opposed them[36] (or nearly 95 per cent of those who knew about the bombings). It is significant that nearly four-fifths of the informed interviewees (60 per cent of the total) believed that expansion of the Vietnam war "might lead to Japan's involvement."

Other nations among the thirty-nine which the State Department says "recognize [through their aid] the importance of success in Vietnam to their own national interest" include Italy, represented by a 9-man surgical team and science scholarships; Belgium, a contribution of medicines; India, clothing for flood relief; Iran, a 22-man medical team and 1,000 tons of petroleum; Laos, $4,167 for flood relief; Israel, pharmaceutical supplies. Such efforts to bind up the wounds of Vietnam in a humanitarian fashion are laudable. But they are certainly not the outpouring of assistance implied in the State Department's claims.

Senator Thruston B. Morton, Republican Senatorial Campaign Committee chairman, at a news conference on October 31, 1966, reported on a private poll on U.S. prestige in Europe which he "had ordered because the Administration has stopped taking soundings where the news is bad." The results, he said, showed that among 6,090 persons polled in Great Britain, West Germany, France, Belgium and Holland "46 per cent felt the United States is moving further away from world peace, while only 14 per cent supported U.S. foreign policy."[37] The day before the Morton statement *The New York Times* headlined an article datelined from Stockholm, "Anti-U.S. Feeling Rising in Sweden—Television and Press Add to Hostility on Vietnam."[38]

Foreign shipping crews on various occasions have refused to help transport U.S. cargo to Vietnam. Indian and Chinese crews aboard British ships have refused. So have Japanese sailors and even Okinawans. "Seven crews," says writer Lester Velie, "turned us down in the space of several weeks."[39]

In the summer of 1965 a cargo slated for a chartered Mexican ship, *El Mexicano*, had a particularly rough time. American longshoremen worked for three days, much of it on overtime, to load the vessel with needed trucks and construction machinery for Vietnam. Only then, ready to sail, did the ship's officers receive a wire notifying them they could not sail without violating Mexican neutrality laws. After unloading *El Mexicano* the longshoremen began transferring the cargo to a Greek ship—but twelve of the Greek crew refused to sail for Vietnam even though they were offered a $10,000 bonus. After two weeks' delay the construction equipment finally sailed on an American ship. Although some freighters have been chartered from NATO allies, some of these countries have at the same time allowed the Russians also to charter their merchantmen, thus freeing Russian ships for the North Vietnam run.

With such attitudes widespread among our allies, it is not surprising that Secretary Rusk came back from the June 1966 Brussels NATO meeting "with little to show for American leadership or general support of U.S. foreign policy . . . the same story [as] the last two previous meetings of NATO."[40] Before he left for that meeting, however, Mr. Rusk had said, "I have found that the objectives of American foreign policy are widely understood, respected and supported," and that "a large majority" of free-world nations are "sympathetic to our efforts in Southeast Asia."

The plain truth is that they are not. Asians closest to the scene want no part of our Vietnam adventure. Three of the seven SEATO nations have not joined the four who are our only allies with troops in Vietnam. Of those four, one (New Zealand) has a token force; a second (Australia) has about one per cent as many troops as the U.S.; and the other two (the Philippines and Korea) are our hired mercenaries.

The reason for the low esteem in which other nations hold us is very simple: they believe for the most part that we are wrong, dead wrong, not only politically but morally, in the role we have adopted in Vietnam. As a Peace Corps volunteer wrote me recently from India, "The people listen to the one community radio in this village and then ask me, 'Why are you bombing poor people like us in Vietnam?' "

The costs of this effort seem clear to me: the loss of lives; the dollar expenditures; the demise of the commitment to fulfill the "promise of American life" at home and to make America *the* example for the world; the mangling of the opportunity to build trust and enhance the cause of peace.

Our returns for these expenditures are: deep divisions among Americans at home; the symptomatic outbreak of violence in our decaying urban areas; the threat of a war widening into World War III; a stalemated war of attrition on the ground in Vietnam; a diversion of our limited resources from the task of eradicating the causes of discontent and violence in the developing nations.

Costs must be measured with results. What are we building in Vietnam? What are we forfeiting by being in Vietnam?

Of course, a policy which protects the American way of life must be maintained by expenses and by assuming risks. However, a crusade to "make the world safe for democracy" or to assure peace by escalating the war against the Viet Cong and the D.R.V. are utopian illusions which are indulged in by "amateurs."

The pursuit by American troops of the work which only the Vietnamese can do for themselves, and obviously have not, is costing America all those values we all hold most dearly.

X

The Morality Gap

Tran, seven years old and the size of an American four-year-old, lay on one of the crowded cots in the stifling fetid August heat of the Qui Nhon provincial hospital. Once a coastal fishing town and French seaside resort of 20,000, now a huge U.S. military supply dump some 300 miles north of Saigon, its estimated population of 200,000 today includes some 72,000 refugees. In the civilian hospital 500 patients lie, like Tran, two or even three to a cot; some of the wounded—four out of six "civilian casualties" are children[1]—arrive too late even to share a bed and lie on stretchers on the floor.

Tran's father was killed in the Vietnamese army. His mother and older brother are somewhere in a refugee camp, but his grandfather, nearly blind with cataracts, is here to look after him. When the bombs fell on their hamlet a week ago the napalm did not get the others, but little Tran, lying quietly now and not crying as he did all week, was deeply burned on his face, his back, and his hand, now stretched out like a starfish. The skin on his little body, writes Martha Gellhorn, "looks like bloody hardened meat in a butcher shop."[2]

The loudspeaker warning for them to leave their village came in the night. The four—mother, grandfather, two boys—got out with two of their precious four buffaloes. But at dawn the grandfather, with Tran to see for him, went back to find the other two. Then the planes came while they were still there, with others likewise returning to salvage more possessions by daylight. The buffaloes—and a good many villagers —were killed by our "improved" napalm, the searing jellied gasoline which clings to and literally melts the flesh. The mother of another seven-year-old from the same hamlet said the Viet Cong guerrillas had come in April "but were long gone; why destroy their houses and possessions and their children now in August?"

There would be no damages for lost property, wounds or death— such payments are for "accidents," but these people had been warned to get out of the way. The old man took the child to the nearest town, and they were flown to Qui Nhon by helicopter. Local authorities and neighbors had given the grandfather 300 piasters when they left, a little more than $2. Here in this hospital no food service is provided, as is usual in South Vietnam's civilian hospitals. The government provides rations for one meal a day for 287 patients at Qui Nhon—but the 500 patients have to be cooked for and cared for by relatives who jam the already packed wards: "grandparents caring for tiny children, teenagers caring for parents, a vast conglomeration of the semi-starved looking after the desperately hurt." After a week Tran's grandfather has only 100 piasters left—when that is gone, what then?

In the preceding chapters, I have concentrated on the political weaknesses of the administration's policy in Vietnam. The seriousness of the dangers which stem from the political errors of this policy is one sound reason for proposing another course of action in Vietnam.

An equally important reason for desiring another policy in Vietnam is the severe damage being done to the American moral position in the council of nations. Both publicly and privately, even our allies have called into question our moral leadership because of the moral results of the administration's policy in Vietnam.

In the past, as a representative of the United States, I have always been extremely moved by the vast reservoir of deeply felt respect for Americans. As a result of American words and American efforts, we have been admired and looked to for moral and humanitarian leadership throughout the world.

The administration's actions in Vietnam have radically altered the traditional image of the United States. The effects of the administration's policy on civilians in Vietnam have caused widespread moral indignation, disgust, and disheartenment among America's friends.

Of course, there has always been an abstract jealousy and resentment over the magnitude of American power and strength. But this does not explain the moral revulsion to the conduct of the administration that has dissipated the previous good feeling around the world for the United States.

The interaction of two considerations has produced the serious deterioration of America's moral position. First, the consequences of the massive application of American technological power against an underdeveloped society have caused many to condemn the morality of the administration as being similar to the morality of Viet Cong terrorists, the only difference being that American power is more destructive. It is difficult for this generation to forget that the only country to employ atomic weapons in wartime was the United States.

Secondly, and just as important, has been the effect on public opinion of the record of explanation by the administration for actions in Vietnam. I have described above the case of civilian casualties resulting from the bombing of North Vietnam as an example of this reaction to the moral position of the administration. First, there were the statements by administration spokesmen that we were hitting only military targets. Then there were charges from Hanoi of civilian casualties. Western reporters in North Vietnam verified the fact that there had been casualties in the North. After a period of repeated denials, dodging, and deceit, the administration finally admitted these facts.

What is the result of carrying out such a policy and then trying to cover it up despite all the evidence to the contrary? Our allies and nonaligned states reason that if the administration admits what the other side has been charging and we were denying for so long, how many more things that the other side is charging are actually being done? If the administration can do these acts in such a deceitful fashion, they ask, then what distinguishes our side from an opponent who also practices and conceals similar treacheries?

The revelations in 1967 of the activities of the Central Intelligence Agency do not buttress the protestations of innocence by the administration. It is precisely this hypocrisy, this attempt to cover over moral ambiguities behind a public relations façade, that has eroded America's moral position.

Professor Robert Osgood has warned us succinctly that "as America's foreign relations grow more complex, there will be a natural tendency to resolve moral dilemmas and contradictions by ignoring them or by rationalizing them out of existence. When the exigencies of national power conflict with universal principles, patriots will tend to reconcile the two goals by identifying American interests with the interests of humanity."[3]

This the administration has done in the case of Vietnam, claiming that there is no moral ambiguity in the execution of American policy there. But the extensive loss of civilian life in the South, the ruthlessness toward civilian possessions and ancestral property, the destruction of a way of life, and the abysmal treatment of the refugees and the sick all belie the rationalizations of the administration and reveal the disgraceful immorality of the American impact on Vietnam. Yet the common American soldier, like his civilian counterpart back home, honestly desires to do good for the South Vietnamese. It is not the individuals but the policy which is causing the terrible consequences.

How many civilian casualties are there, by any reasonable estimate, in South Vietnam?

In 1966 an increasing number of accounts by reporters, doctors, and visitors describing refugees and casualties began to appear, mostly in the more liberal, and critical, press. The Subcommittee on Refugees of the Senate Judiciary Committee began its investigation of the problem. It was April 1967 before the U.S. Mission in Saigon released for the first time official figures on civilian casualties treated in South Vietnam's 150 hospitals and dispensaries.

According to those figures, the largest number of civilian casualties treated during one month in 1964 was 1,400, rising to 1,566 in 1965. In December 1966, 2,500 civilians were treated for war-related injuries; 4,150 in January 1967, and 3,920 in February.[4] Later, in July, the Saigon government said 21,112 wounded civilians had been treated in the first six months of 1967, an average of 3,500 per month.[5]

Now, how can we reconstruct from these figures the actual number of civilian casualties which are being inflicted in this war?

First, members of the Refugee Subcommittee staff told *The New York Times* that "they had reason to believe, as a result of their investigation, that the statistics [of our own Mission] were incomplete because some hospitals were not included and the number of civilian casualties admitted to others was understated."[6]

Second, the statistics embrace only areas with access to government-controlled hospitals. As Richard Harwood wrote in the *Washington Post*, "the presumption is that heavier casualties are sustained in Viet Cong areas than in areas under Saigon's control because of the persistent bombing and artillery attacks on those areas."[7] As a working hypothesis, a conservative estimate would be that there is at least one casualty in N.L.F. controlled areas for every casualty in areas under Allied control.

Third, how many of the wounded actually reach the medical centers? Because transportation is difficult, wounded civilians as a rule require 36 to 48 hours to reach medical help.[8] Senator Edward Kennedy, Refugee Subcommittee chairman, says it is "the virtually unanimous view of the medical personnel, both here and in Vietnam, that only one out of two or perhaps even one out of three civilian casualties actually reached these medical facilities."[9]

Helicopter evacuation of our wounded and our remarkable military medical system have resulted in saving nearly six out of seven Americans wounded in Vietnam. In South Vietnam's army, however, the figure is more nearly one death for every two wounded—4,718 killed and 10,114 wounded in the first half of 1967.[10] Let us assume, conservatively, the same ratio among civilians. What conclusions can be drawn from all this?

Fourth, what is the relationship between the number wounded and the number of civilians who are killed? We know from the figures of the army of South Vietnam that for every two wounded there is one who is killed. Given the remoteness of medical facilities from the wounded civilians, the length of time it takes for the civilian to reach these facilities, and the inadequacies of the medical services available for civilians in contrast to those of the military, I am going to use the estimate of 1.5 wounded equal to 1 killed. Again, I feel that this is conservative and and that perhaps a more realistic estimate would be a one-to-one ratio.

What understanding can we reach through the employment of the figures and the considerations discussed above? We can start with a base figure of 4,500 reported and treated civilian wounded each month. This figure reflects the increased tempo of the war and the errors in reporting from the hospitals to the central government. It equals a rate of 54,000 per year.

Let us recall the difficulties in getting to one of these centers and the fact that the heavier bombardment of N.L.F. areas is not reflected in this figure. Therefore, it seems reasonable to conclude that for every wounded person receiving treatment there is at least one wounded person who is not treated. Now we have a total of about 105,000 civilian wounded each year.

If there are 105,000 wounded, then following the wounded and killed ratio in the army of South Vietnam and the consideration mentioned above, we must conclude that there are around 60,000 to 70,000 civilians killed per year in addition to the 105,000 wounded. The total of civilian casualties in 1967 would appear to be in the neighborhood of 175,000, caused by both sides in the fighting.

What does this figure mean?

In the first half of 1967, there were 14,828 casualties in the army of South Vietnam, 4,714 killed and 10,114 wounded. The rate for 1967 would be a total of 30,000 casualties in the army.

These figures on civilian casualties mean, then, that *there are over five civilian casualties for every one military casualty currently being suffered among the South Vietnamese.*

Has the administration ever honestly, from the beginning, told the American people that this tremendous cost would be a part of saving the South Vietnamese? Is this impact of the administration's policy on the people of South Vietnam one that can make us all proud to be Americans? Does the administration have a morality gap that is as wide as that of the Viet Cong terrorists?

If the American people do not comprehend the effect of American military power on the people of Vietnam, we can be certain that the Vietnamese people themselves do. That the people of South Vietnam better understand the effects of American military power on the civilian populace can be clearly seen from their responses to a CBS-backed public opinion poll taken in South Vietnam.

Only 37 per cent responded affirmatively when they were asked if they thought the United States should continue to bombard villages in which the Viet Cong were believed to be hiding. On another question, only 15 per cent felt that the U.S. should rely on military efforts against North Vietnam, while 63 per cent wanted the U.S. to increase efforts aimed at negotiations with North Vietnam. Finally, a related question asked the people of South Vietnam what their first wish for Vietnam was: 4 per cent replied that it was for a victory over communism, 81 per cent replied that it was for peace.[11]

We can be certain that these questions would have produced an even stronger response in favor of de-escalation by the United States if they could have been asked of the civilians who live in the territory of the N.L.F.

These figures do help us to understand certain realities of life, death, and injury among the civilians in South Vietnam. However, no figures can measure some of the other moral problems raised by the use of massive firepower in South Vietnam. How can one measure the meaning of the destruction of a way of life for these people with their values of ancestor worship, their attachment to the land? How can one measure the foul conditions which the ever growing numbers of refugees from military action are currently being forced to endure? How will these conditions ever endear the vast bulk of the population to the Saigon regime, much less convince them to participate in this struggle on the side of Saigon?

In all of South Vietnam there are about 100 civilian hospitals with 25,000 beds—one for every 600 inhabitants of the country. There are about 800 South Vietnamese doctors—but 500 of them are in the army and 150 make a good living treating only private patients who can afford their fees. That leaves 150 government doctors, or about one for every 100,000 citizens.[12] According to former Health Minister Dr. Ba Kha there are about 9 nurses and 5 midwives per 100,000.

Some hospitals are staffed and run by foreigners, such as the Adventist Hospital in Saigon, so overcrowded that some patients "were lying on a stone slab in the scrub room—delivery cases";[13] and the country's only children's hospital, run by the Swiss-based international organization Terre des Hommes. There, as in other hospitals, many of the 600 patients in a 220-bed institution lie on newspapers for lack of sheets. "In other hospitals, some newspapers and wrapping paper are commonly used as dressing for burns, being the only material available."

The 350-bed Da Nang Surgical Hospital, according to a volunteer American medical intern there in the summer of 1966, "never had fewer than 700 patients," 80 per cent of them suffering from injuries inflicted by American or South Vietnamese action. With 100 burn patients a month, the intern (David McLanahan, one of five under a U.S. AID program) reported that during his whole time there the hospital had only one half-pint jar of antibiotic cream—brought in privately by a surgeon and saved for "children who had a chance of recovery." Sixty to seventy per cent of the patients were under 12 years old.

The Surgical Hospital, "probably as well off as any Vietnamese hospital outside Saigon," uses outdated blood from military hospitals, but most others are chronically short of blood. A Terre des Hommes report says: "In places with the atmosphere of slaughter houses for people, where flies circulate freely on children who have been skinned alive, there are no facilities for hygiene, no fans, and no air conditioning." In some places short of intravenous fluids there is resort to an expedient reportedly often practiced by the Viet Cong—sticking a tube into a coconut for its uncontaminated glucose-like fluid. The Ministry of Health receives, for all of South Vietnam's public health needs, less than 1 per cent of the national budget.

Dedicated Americans are trying to help. According to the Komer report,[14] 153 American doctors from 38 states under "Project Vietnam" had completed two-month voluntary tours at Vietnamese provincial hospitals, and 42 "free world" medical teams, half being American military personnel, were at work in civilian hospitals.

"The U.S." says the report by White House Special Assistant Komer, "has donated 28 *surgical suites* to hospitals throughout the country" [original italics]. The Refugee Subcommittee of the Senate report published six months earlier confirms this: "There are 28 provincial hospitals in South Vietnam in which surgical suites have been constructed." Then it adds what the Komer report fails to mention: "Only 11 of these hospitals were being used [during the Committee's visit] because additional medical personnel were unavailable."[15]

At Qui Nhon, the New Zealand doctor whose medical team runs the hospital told Martha Gellhorn, "AID spent $2 millions on fixing up this hospital"—and showed her "a small smoke-blackened cavern [which] was the hospital kitchen, flanked by six latrines. Four were boarded up, totally blocked by excrement; two open doors showed overflowing mounds of filth. 'Facilities for the families,' the doctor said."

Across the way was a handsome new building put up by AID for the relatives of patients. "Marvelous dining room," the doctor said, "screened, never used; they take food to their wounded and eat whatever's left over, squatting on the floor the way they always have." A bedroom, too, where "maybe 30 could sleep in it cheek by jowl"—but the 600 relatives sleep on the floor "beside their own people, have to, who else is to look after the patients at night?"[16]

"More Vietnamese," says the Komer report enthusiastically, "now have better access to medical care than ever before in their lives." Nevertheless the fact remains that an estimated 30 per cent of Vietnamese have tuberculosis and 80 per cent suffer from one or another variety of worms.[17]

How Saigon's hospital funds are allocated sometimes depends on politics. A leading doctor in the I Corps area has difficulty getting supplies for his hospital because he is suspected in Saigon of having been sympathetic to the Buddhist movement that rocked the area. In Hué, where some of the faculty and students of the medical school were Buddhist sympathizers, "the school and [1,500-bed] hospital receive absolutely no medical supplies from Saigon; only aid from the West German government keeps it operating at all."

By arrangement with Dr. Ba Kha, Terre des Hommes brought 32 children out of Vietnam in May 1966—at about $1,500 per child for air fare, since their appeal to the U.S. government for help was turned down—to hospitals in Europe, where 400 beds and the services of surgeons had been donated. The sick and wounded children included eight burn victims, one of them an eight-year-old boy wearing a muslin bag over his face as he left the plane, so horrible were his burns. "His parents had been burned alive. His chin had 'melted' into his throat, so that he could not close his mouth. He had no eyelids. After the injury he had had no treatment—none whatever—for four months." Now, although he will need a dozen operations, he has been given eyelids and he can close his mouth.

In September a representative of the organization picked another 26 children for a flight to Geneva—but when they arrived they were not the ones originally selected. All were chronically ill polio, cardiac, and cerebral-spastic children; not one was a war victim. Dr. Ba Kha had been replaced; the first group "had caused a tremendous stir about the cruel effect of the bombing." Obviously someone had decided that it was poor public relations for the outside world to get a firsthand look at napalm burns and cruelly injured child victims from South Vietnam.

How many of these children have American (and their own government's) actions killed or injured?

Hugh Campbell, the Canadian former International Control Commission member, has said that from 1961 through 1963 Vietnamese civilians killed in the war were 160,000, a figure accepted by Saigon. Estimates put the 1964 figure at 55,000, and those of 1965 and 1966 at about 100,000 each—conservative figures—for a total of at least 415,000 civilian deaths. Another 100,000 for 1967 brings the total to more than half a million.[18] According to a UNESCO study of 1964, children under 16 comprise 47.5 per cent of Vietnam's population. But in the rural villages where most of the bombs fall, with nearly all able-bodied males above 16 fighting on one side or the other, the ratio of children usually reaches some 70 per cent. *Thus at least a quarter of a million of these dead were children.*

The enormity of this carnage has not been made known to the American public. We read of bomb strikes and our natural assumption is that our planes are hitting at enemy soldiers. But this is a different kind of war, in which "enemies" and "friendlies" are often difficult to distinguish.

We appear to have adopted at times a "scorched earth" policy of absolute destruction of civilian areas in a complete and total manner rarely if ever seen in modern times. Bernard Fall, writing from the scene, graphically described the January 1967 drive on the "Iron Triangle," in which the town of Ben Suc with "3,500 women, children and old men (there was not one able-bodied man in the lot)" was leveled by torch and bulldozer. This 19-day Operation Cedar Falls, described as "the largest military drive of the war" to that date, took the homes of some 6,000 civilians in all with the intention of making the area unusable for the Viet Cong by smashing their tunnels and destroying their supplies. But within a week the VC were back to attack a U.S. infantry platoon on "security duty" in the very same area; they "inflicted heavy casualties," a term indicating that the unit was wiped out as a fighting force.[19]

"Inexorably," wrote Professor Fall, "the bulldozers bit into the countryside, cutting huge swaths of cleared land right across the Triangle. They were followed by flamethrower tanks and teams on foot, destroying the felled trees with fire. And not only the trees: every human habitation within the beaten zone, be it an isolated hut which may have been used by the Viet Cong, or a whole little hamlet inhabited for years by charcoal kilners—non-white Saigon cooks with charcoal almost exclusively—went up in flames. . . . [The people] went without offering resistance, believing that they would merely be taken away temporarily until the operation was over. But . . . there would be no coming back, because Ben Suc would be put to the torch and then razed with bulldozers, just like the forest and part of the rubber plantation."[20]

Such operations add vast numbers of refugees to the toll of civilian victims. They have not lost their lives, but they have lost their homes and most of their possessions, have been forced into unfamiliar surroundings, and deprived of their normal livelihood. We, with our American mobility, cannot comprehend the attachment of the peasant to his soil, his hamlet, his village. An ancestor worshiper (whether a Confucianist or nominal Buddhist), his parents and grandparents are buried here; this is the house and these the fruit trees they knew. It may have taken him a lifetime to build his own house, or it may have been built by father or grandfather; now it is all gone, nothing left. Will the peasants' undying gratitude be won by a government which does this to them? Or are we making new Communist sympathizers by such means? As Colonel Nguyen Khuong, former South Vietnamese military attaché in Washington who now teaches Vietnamese to Americans, put it in a press conference protesting the Iron Triangle operation, "When we move them we ruin them."[21] Col. Khuong should know—he was Inspector General of Diem's "strategic hamlet" program.

In September 1967 Don Luce resigned as director of the International Volunteer Service in Vietnam. A veteran of nine years in the country, he was joined by three other I.V.S. officials in resigning and by 50 other I.V.S. volunteers in a letter to President Johnson. In a statement published in The New York Times on September 24, 1967 Mr. Luce spoke out strongly: "What's going on here is changing these people and it's overwhelming. In 1958 and 1959 you would walk into a village and they would invite you in and talk to you and tell you what was on their minds. Now you walk into a village and the people walk into their houses. When you talk to them they reply with only one thing: what can you give me, what can you offer me. These people have changed. It's become unbearable to witness the destruction of Vietnamese family life, the home, the agricultural system, the transportation. We're defeating ourselves here."[22]

At the beginning of 1965, the number of refugees was some 200,000. By September it had reached 600,000 and by the end of 1965 there were a million South Vietnamese war refugees.[23] It is estimated that in 1966 the number grew to a million and a half—no one really knows just how many there are; current estimates run as high as four million. But it was February 1966 before the South Vietnamese government established the post of Special Commissioner for Refugees—until then refugee care had been divided among several ministries. Registered refugees (and there are vast numbers not registered) receive about 8 cents a day (10 piasters) or 4 cents and 400 grams of rice. The typical refugee camp contains "a series of long hut-like buildings," says the Senate Subcommittee on Refugees, "divided into single rooms with dirt floors, bamboo sides, and aluminum roofing. Health conditions were poor. Sanitation facilities and the water supply were often inadequate. . . . Few schools exist for refugee children, and apparently no educational program was being planned for these children." In fact, only 10 to 20 per cent of all South Vietnam's children are in school.

Martha Gellhorn[24] describes vividly her visit to a refugee camp a few miles outside Saigon, reached by a muddy path after the way became impassable for a car. "On acres of an old dump heap," she writes, "rows and rows of sagging tiny shacks appeared to be floating on mud and green stagnant water. Lesser rows of unfinished cement-brick houses flanked the shacks. The acrid smell of garbage lingered in the air." The only water available was either from the rains or by purchase and carrying.

Never until the war in Vietnam has any nation so deliberately, extensively, and systematically destroyed a people's food supplies as we are doing there. Beginning in November 1961,[25] the spraying of "weed-killer chemicals (2,4-D and 2,4,5-T) from low-flying planes with 1,000-gallon spray tanks—enough to cover 300 acres—was adopted as a means of denuding the jungle in narrow strips alongside routes suspected of harboring concealed troop movements. But by 1963 these chemicals were being sprayed on cropland to cause food shortages in

Viet Cong-held areas—an ironic activity in the face of the world's need and the humanitarian efforts of the United States and the United Nations otherwise to feed starving people in food-short areas.[26]

By late 1965, the seven C-123 planes—since increased to eighteen —of "Operation Ranch Hand" were "using enough chemical to cover about 20,000 acres a month" in their crop-duster-type flights, spreading the "winter in Vermont" look over jungle and cropland. By then 50,000 to 75,000 acres of cultivated land were reported affected.[27] Six months later another Saigon dispatch put the blight of "rice and other food plants" at about 130,000 acres, an area ten times the size of Manhattan, with 59,000 acres of the total the result of operations in the first half of 1966 alone. The cumulative figure of destruction for both jungle and cropland in 1965 and six months of 1966 was reported as 640,000 acres, or 1,000 square miles—almost as much as the total area of Rhode Island or the total farm land of Connecticut.[28] In the months since, with the operation further stepped up, many thousands of additional acres have surely been blasted. As a waggish sign in Operation Ranch Hand headquarters puts it, "Only You Can Prevent a Forest."

According to "Compensation for Crop Losses," a leaflet supposed to be dropped over target areas before attack, "the Government [of South Vietnam] will compensate for all the damage done to your rice crop; meanwhile the Government will at all times help to evacuate you to other places with food, lodging and clothing provided until the next harvesting season, if you so desire."[29] But in order to secure damages the farmer must submit a claim form to the hamlet chief, from where it goes to the village office, then to the provincial office and from there to the province agricultural service. If verified, the claim finally goes to the central government for approval of payment, then back to the provincial office for settlement. Obviously not many peasants get paid for their loss; only a comparative few even file claims. On the other hand, if claims are made for destruction of rubber trees from a French-owned plantation such as that visited by Sanche de Gramont[30] inside VC-held territory, "prompt action is taken to pay damages. The current price for a mature rubber tree is $87."[31] At the same time, we have paid compensation for a villager's life taken by accidental bombing or shelling of civilians in a friendly area at about a third of that amount—$33. Surely it must be grist for the Communist propaganda mill to be able to charge that we value a human life at $33 and a rubber tree at $87.

One of the chemicals in our "tear gas" arsenal is CNS, a compound which includes chloroform and chloropicrin. "Even in small doses it may cause considerable crying, nausea, colic and diarrhea that may persist for weeks."[32] It may be dispensed from bombs, spray tanks, mortar shells, and grenades.

Similar symptoms are described as the effects of arsenic compounds, which include Lewisite gas: immediate nausea, vomiting, acute headache, and cumulative effects which include hair falling out, visual impairment and possible bilateral blindness, confusion and hallucination. Both CNS and arsenic compounds have been listed among "chemical agents explicitly developed by the United States for use in South Vietnam" and "currently in use in South Vietnam according to admissions of U.S. officials, or reports of responsible western journalists, or both."[33] Deputy Secretary of Defense Cyrus R. Vance, for example, was asked at a National Foreign Policy Conference in Washington in October 1965 if the United States was using arsenic and cyanide in Vietnam. He answered: "We are making limited use of them in the southern part of Vietnam but not yet in the North."[34]

The history of escalation, as I have said before, is that it breeds more escalation. It is to be feared that the use of chemical and biological weapons is no more immune to that process than other types of warfare. It is that fear which spurred a worldwide outcry when it was initially disclosed that "some temporarily disabling 'types of tear gas' for combat" had been employed in late 1964 and early 1965, though not reported until March 1965. "As far as is known," said a *New York Times* report then, "this was the first time that the United States was involved in the combat use of gas since World War. I."[35]

The admitted sequence has been a movement from defoliation of useless jungle to destruction of crops—on an ever-increasing scale— to use of "disabling" gases claimed to be nonlethal. Nevertheless, it is on record that in one case six Australians entering a tunnel after the use of gas *while wearing gas masks* were made ill—and one of them died of the effects.[36] The next tempting step in the escalation of CBW (chemical and biological warfare) would be to dip into our arsenal of more deadly resources to step up further what U Thant has called "this barbarous war." Over the past two years several articles have appeared, written by military men or reflecting the opinion of some of them, which argue that rather than submitting to world opinion on the subject, we should increasingly use chemical and biological warfare as a matter of policy—on the ground that it is a more humane (and less costly) way of fighting.

What do we have in our CBW arsenal? What might escalation perhaps lead us to use? I raise the question of our CBW arsenal because the facts are not common public knowledge and because its use, or potential use, has a direct bearing on the morality of our policy. As a supporter of the Freedom of Information law which went into effect July 4, 1967, I believe America is better served by keeping the actions of all government agencies under a constant floodlight as far as possible.

General J. A. Rothschild, retired Commanding General of the U.S. Army Chemical Corps Research and Development Command, is an enthusiast for CBW agents, which he calls *Tomorrow's Weapons* in the title of his 1964 book. In fighting guerrillas he recommends "the use of toxics," especially "air-borne agents, either lethal or incapacitating." "Insect vectors," "anti-animal biological agents," and "anti-crop agents" as well as anti-personnel agents would be useful, in his opinion. He devotes a chapter to "Food as a target for toxic attack," in which he finds "biological anti-crop agents" superior to chemicals; fungi such as cereal rust, potato blight, and rice blast are good possibilities. He includes maps dealing with the problems of germ and gas dispersion, among them one of Russia and two showing "Airflow from Siberian Polar Air Mass Over China" and "Summer Monsoonal Airflow Over China." An appendix details thirty-two "diseases of possible biological warfare interest," including botulism, cholera, encephalitis, plague, and tularemia.[37]

There has been a great increase in recent years in the amount of CBW research in the United States. The newest chemicals, not yet used so far as is known but already stockpiled and available, are "nerve gases"—good candidates for the next level of this kind of escalation. Two of these, GB and VX, are among the seven chemical agents now in our arsenal, standardized for use and listed in the military field manual FM 3-10, *Employment of Chemical and Biological Agents*. GB, or Sarin, is the American improvement on GA (Tabun), developed by the Germans but not used in World War II.

An article in the magazine *Missiles and Rockets* describes nerve gas as "the most deadly of chemical weapons."[38] The deadliness of CBW weapons is stated in terms of "median lethal dose" (LD_{50}): the quantity of the agent needed to kill half the persons exposed to it. This dose is expressed as the number of milligrams per cubic meter of air which would kill in one minute (mg-min/m^3). Thus for Sarin the LD_{50} is 25 mg-min/m^3 for active men. To put it into more understandable terms, if you had a dozen people in a 12-by-15-foot room with a 9-foot ceiling, six would be dead in one minute if the total amount of Sarin in the air (assuming uniform distribution) came to *one four-hundredth of an ounce*.[39]

"Under field concentrations of 10 times the median lethal dosage," says the article, "easily obtained in small areas for a short time, one inward breath of Sarin would kill." Colorless, odorless, and tasteless, the chemical breaks down an enzyme (acetylcholinesterase) by which nerves control muscle action. The result is that all the muscles now try to operate at once, fighting each other; respiration and heart action cannot continue under such severe fibrillation. Skin absorption of Sarin, though not quite so instant-acting, has the same effect. Sarin is one of the chemicals "produced and loaded into rockets, land mines and artillery shells" at a plant which I have visited in my home state. Located at Newport, Indiana, and operated by the Food Machinery Corporation at an annual cost of $3.5 million, its 300 employees have kept it operating 24 hours a day since 1960.[40]

General Rothschild is a proponent not only of chemicals for warfare, but of bacteriological agents as well. Plague, the notorious "black death" of the Middle Ages, is one of the diseases he finds worth considering—although for sabotage he prefers botulinum toxin as "an ideal agent." The manner of thinking of CBW devotees is indicated when, in his professional way, he puts those "ideal" qualities thus: "Botulism has a death rate of 60 to 70 per cent, an incubation period of 12 to 36 hours, and susceptibility is general. It has the additional advantage that immunization methods are available to protect the saboteurs, while there is not really adequate treatment for the disease." In short, "botulism is . . . an ideal disease to use in this particular case. . . ."[41]

Our chief center for research on such arcane matters is Fort Detrick, a complex of $75,000,000 worth of buildings on 1,300 acres near Frederick, Maryland. Much of Detrick's work in microorganisms has "an inverted quality like that of medicine turned inside out . . . [including] efforts to breed into pathogenic organisms precisely the characteristics—such as resistance to antibiotics—that medical researchers would like to see eradicated."[42] The scientific staff includes 12 Ph.D.'s and 14 M.D.'s, and among more than a dozen diseases which are "the objects of considerable research" are botulism toxin, plague, and tularemia. Only 15 per cent of their findings are published other than in "a secret literature managed by the Department of Defense" available only to agencies and contractors on a "need to know" basis. (Among the contractors are a number of universities.) Plant and animal as well as human diseases are under study here: a Detrick researcher in 1965 received the Army's Distinguished Service Medal—its highest civilian award—for her developments in rice blast fungus, a disease which "has repeatedly damaged Asian rice crops."

At least as early as 1959, Fort Detrick researchers were working with the virulent pneumonic plague, which does not rely on the rat-and-flea cycle for its spread—inhaling of droplets from a sneeze or cough will do it.

In late February 1968 the World Health Organization reported that plague had struck at least 7,000 persons in Vietnam in the last two years, with at least 200 deaths—"95 per cent of all the plague cases in the world." The extremely deadly pneumonic plague "cropped up in Vietnam less than two years ago—the first reported case of the dread disease in Vietnam in 25 years. Since the first case, 57 new cases of pneumonic plague have occurred in Vietnam, said WHO." Of the six forms of plague, all were reported now found in 27 of the 47 South Vietnam provinces. In addition, cholera was considered by WHO to be "just as serious as plague," with 1,100 suspected deaths out of 38,000 suspected cases in Vietnam between January 1, 1964 and November 24, 1967. WHO "blamed the sudden rise of plague in war-ravaged Vietnam on the disruption and the massive movements of refugees in the war zones of Vietnam."[43]

The continuation of experiments with plague is evidenced by an article appearing in *Science* in July 1965 by three Detrick researchers. Tables show the median lethal dose for three different strains of the plague bacillus (*Pasteurella pestis*) when given to "normal and treated mice" by three different methods of injection—in the blood stream, in the abdominal cavity, and under the skin. Just *ten individual microbes* are enough to cause death in some circumstances.[44]

In mid-July 1965 reports were circulating that the Defense Department had contracted with Travelers' Research Corporation of Hartford "to adapt bubonic plague for aerial dissemination in Vietnam."[45] Says a recent brochure by the company: "The extensive experience of the TRC staff in research on turbulent diffusion and transport of atmospheric contaminants provides a firm base for TRC's participation in the nation's CB weapons analysis program."[46] However, the existence of a specific bubonic plague development contract was categorically denied by State Department and Defense officials in responding to queries by members of an organization of doctors, "Physicians for Social Responsibility," which had raised the question.

Their concern led to inquiries by Drew Pearson and Jack Anderson, in the course of which "a high level State Department official and a White House aide . . . confirmed the reports on germ warfare, but added that it was not bubonic plague but tularemia which was being developed. The White House aide indicated that a final decision to use this weapon had not yet been made, but that there was a good chance it would be used and spread in such a way as to enable U.S. forces to deny responsibility, saying instead it was a naturally occurring epidemic."[47] According to the same source, a mid-June 1965 State Department memo to the President reversed State's long-standing opposition to use of such weapons.

I am not saying that we *have* used biological weapons in Vietnam, whether plague or tularemia or any other microbes. But it is a fact that we are carrying out extensive research at a stepped-up pace. In fiscal 1961 the research and development budget for chemical and biological warfare was about $57 million; but in 1964 it was up to $158 million, and remains at about that level.[48] In addition to research there is the amount spent on procurement, a sum which has been classified in recent years.

To sum up: even more damaging than the credibility gap is what might be called America's "morality gap" in Vietnam. A nation cannot furnish moral leadership while performing immoral acts. This is at the heart of my objection to what we are doing in Vietnam—it is basically immoral. Supposed political expediency can never justify clear-cut immorality whether in national or international politics. It may appear to succeed in the short term, but it carries the seeds of self-destruction.

XI

Principles for a Peace Policy

The growing involvement of the United States in the war in Vietnam has engendered a serious and far-reaching debate in the United States. This debate is being undertaken to determine precisely where we are now and what we must do in order to achieve a peace in Southeast Asia that will preserve the vital interests of our country and the traditional values that constitute the greatness of America.

As I stated in the Introduction, it is incumbent upon each concerned citizen and every elected representative to participate fully in this process of democratic decision-making. It is incumbent upon each individual to present his analysis of the realities that confront the United States. From an understanding of these realities, one can formulate the principles for our foreign policy which can best fulfill the high promises that America has set for herself and for humanity.

In order to meet these responsibilities, I have publicly advised against the pursuit of the policy of escalation since its inception in February 1965. Because of these responsibilities, because of the logical fallacies in the policy of escalation, and because there are so many demanding problems in the world to which America should be giving her attention, I have written this book.

I have covered in detail the many facets of the American crisis in Vietnam as I see them. The war continues and the killing continues to increase. The policy of the administration has not been able to achieve a settlement of this conflict. There is no peace in Asia or any hope of peace in Asia in the foreseeable future as long as the present policy is followed.

The history of this policy has been the history of a widening war. Given the fact that there is no hope of a settlement, given the fact that the trend of the policy of escalation is that of a widening war, then we see that this local, widening war in Vietnam contains the possibility of becoming a general world war.

The war in Vietnam is a crisis for the Vietnamese people and a crisis for the world. As a result of the war in Vietnam, there is also a crisis among the American people. A public opinion survey in October 1967 revealed that only 28 per cent of the American people support the policy of the administration.[1] The American people are dissatisfied. The American people are divided.

Americans want to know, need to know, where do we go from here? What is the alternative to continuing the present policy? How can a peace be achieved in Southeast Asia which is consonant with the vital interests of the United States? What is the solution to the American Crisis in Vietnam? What is the way out of the American Crisis in Vietnam?

I believe that there is a way out of the American Crisis in Vietnam. How can we find the basis for the settlement of this crisis? The first step is to analyze the exact nature of the policy of the administration. What is this policy attempting to achieve? Why is the policy not attaining its goal? What are the defects in the policy? After we comprehend the exact nature of this policy and its shortcomings, then we can set forth in a direction that can take us out of the American Crisis in Vietnam.

One basic principle of American policy in Vietnam prior to February 1965 was not to become involved in a land war in Asia. Since that date, the administration's policy of escalation has taken us into precisely that land war. Below is a review of the characteristics of the policy of escalation which have been developed in detail in this book. First we must understand this policy and its weaknesses, why it is failing to protect the best interests and to implement the best values of the United States. From this understanding we can then determine the *principles* of a foreign policy that will be in the vital interests of the United States and provide a basis for the settlement of the crisis in Vietnam.

1. *The public decision was sound in 1964 when the elections mandated "no wider war."*

In the Presidential campaign of 1964 the American people were offered a clear choice between two courses. One said that the use of American military force could solve the problems which confront us, even though these problems were primarily political. The American people massively sustained the other alternative, the alternative presented by President Johnson as the Democratic candidate for election to the office he had inherited on the death of President Kennedy. He said then, "Others are eager to enlarge the conflict. They call upon us to supply American boys to do the job that Asian boys should do. They ask us to take reckless action which would risk the lives of millions, engulf much of Asia, and threaten the peace of the entire world. Such action would offer no solution to the real problem of Vietnam."[2]

From the decisive choice of the people in this election, it was clear that they favored the principle of American foreign policy which stood against the indiscriminate use of military power as a solution to the basic problems of Vietnam. The course of the war in Vietnam has since disastrously proven the validity of this principle: the gradual increase in the use of American force to a massive and reckless level cannot offer a "solution to the real problem of Vietnam."

2. *The policy of escalation has not only engaged American soldiers in a land war in Asia—the policy of escalation has Americanized the war.*

Americans have been substituted to do the jobs which South Vietnamese have failed to do. When Americans do these jobs, South Vietnamese are not doing them. They will never do them as long as the Americans are there to do the work for them and to die for them. As long as the enemies of the Saigon government know that the Saigon regime is not a real or effective government, they will continue to fight.

3. *The impact of the policy of escalation upon South Vietnam has been to disrupt that society.*

The introduction of American money has reinforced the corruption of public officials in South Vietnam and thereby undermined any dedication they might have had to the war effort. Further, emphasis on military firepower has subordinated political considerations in the South, turning at least one out of every seven South Vietnamese into a refugee. The high rate of civilian casualties has caused hatred and disillusionment among the civilian populace.

Not only is this a failure to build a better way of life for the South Vietnamese people, not only is this a contradiction of what I believe America should stand for, but there is an even more serious consequence: The disruption of South Vietnam's society provides the breeding ground on which the Viet Cong thrive.

After over 100,000 American casualties, what are the fruits of the policy of escalation? When that policy was initiated in early 1965, there were about 100,000 Viet Cong in South Vietnam. In the fall of 1967 there were an estimated 300,000 enemy soldiers in the field. By mid-1967, after five pacification programs within the decade, only 1,944 of the 12,357 hamlets in South Vietnam were classified as under partial or total government control.[3]

4. Escalation breeds escalation.

Each time the use of force has not convinced the other side to give in, more force has been applied. In response the other side has matched the escalation with an escalation of its own. Now almost the only thing left to escalate against in the North is the people, the society of North Vietnam. Do we want the United States to stand for the destruction of a civilian population? Do we have any illusions that the allies of North Vietnam will acquiesce in that destruction?

5. Another consequence of the policy of escalation has been the brutalization of humanity.

This is one of the cruelest wars in the history of man. Both sides are guilty, each in its own way, of trampling upon those human values which all Americans cherish. The "morality gap" is enormous, and on moral grounds alone we ought to find a speedy solution.

This is not what I believe America has to offer to the disadvantaged people of the world. But this *is* what the policy of escalation is making America stand for. Professor Hans Morgenthau has called it the "violence of impotence." Because violence and brutality are going on in Vietnam, they can more easily be applied here in America.

6. A cost of the policy of escalation is the vast number of lives being lost, both Americans and South Vietnamese.

These losses cannot be measured in any quantitative terms. Only the people who are left behind know the void in their lives which has been caused by the policy of escalation and the failure to achieve peace. Since almost nothing is being achieved for the people of South Vietnam, it is impossible to justify these losses.

7. The policy of escalation carries a high monetary cost.

What are we building, what returns are we getting for our expenditure in Vietnam of an amount equal to all of the outlays by the American government from its founding through 1917?

8. Escalation in Vietnam has meant the death of the Great Society.

In 1964 the administration promised the American people that it would begin the long-needed reconstruction and improvement of our society at home. This effort would have taken a huge allocation of both effort and monetary resources. We cannot have the war in Vietnam as a constant drain and at the same time commit the resources necessary to cope with our domestic needs.

9. *The policy of escalation has exacerbated our problems with China, not to mention Russia.*

Secretary Rusk has a dire prophecy about the future plans of "a billion Chinese armed with nuclear weapons." I do not know if China will be an expansionist power five years from now. I do know that the Chinese now are verbally truculent, but that this truculence should not mislead us, because the Chinese have acted conservatively. However, the policy of escalation can very easily become a self-fulfilling prophecy by goading the Chinese into an aggressive response. The policy of escalation is not strengthening the hand of the moderates in China who believe that the United States and China can co-exist without nuclear war.

10. *Finally, the policy of escalation in Vietnam has been carried out in direct violation of our pledged word in the United Nations charter.*

The principles which the Charter embodies for the peaceful settlement of international disputes are the best hope that we have for building a workable world order that can help to preserve peace. If we do not follow those principles, we cannot demand that others do so. I cannot support a policy of escalation that transforms these fundamental basic commitments into mere "scraps of paper."

These characteristics of the policy of escalation demonstrate why that policy cannot meet the real problems in South Vietnam and cannot effect a solution to that conflict. In other words, these are all negative results of the policy of escalation. However, *there is one affirmative result of the policy of escalation—it has produced conditions in South Vietnam which appear to verify the original justification for resorting to that policy of escalation.*

Ward Just, *Washington Post* bureau chief in Saigon, has said, "The Viet Cong met the Saigon government in a reasonably fair test of aims and ideals in the late 1950's and early 1960's and for all practical purposes won."[4] They were able to do so because the grievances of the people of South Vietnam were real, allowing the Viet Cong to accumulate sufficient strength to defeat the Saigon regime had we not intervened with escalation.

But the administration has a different version as to why the policy of escalation was originally adopted. Secretary Rusk said in October 1967, "We did not put our combat forces into South Vietnam because of dissident elements in South Vietnam. We put our combat forces in there because North Vietnamese forces moved into South Vietnam. So that our problem of peace is with Hanoi."[5]

What is the evidence for this charge of "armed aggression from the North" which served as the justification for the policy of escalation? The State Department White Paper of February 1965 was able to document the existence of six North Vietnamese infiltrators in South Vietnam. In May 1965 Secretary McNamara said that evidence had been gathered showing the existence of "400 to 500" North Vietnamese troops in South Vietnam in March 1965—a month after bombing of the North began. At the same time there were over 20,000 American troops in South Vietnam.

When Rusk said in his news conference in October 1967 that "there are North Vietnamese regiments today fighting in South Vietnam," he was of course absolutely correct. But we have seen that the Secretary is confused—he has taken the *results* of the policy of escalation and used them as *proof* for the original charge of aggression. The Secretary wants to lead us away from the fact that *the policy of escalation has produced conditions in South Vietnam which appear to verify the original justification for resorting to that policy of escalation.* It is precisely this result of escalation—the existence of North Vietnamese troops in the South—that allows the administration to persist in this brutal, costly and dangerous policy of escalation.

There is another fundamental error in the conception of the policy of the administration. In blaming the policy of escalation on the need to defeat "aggression from the North," the administration is neglecting two crucial considerations. First, nothing has ever been accomplished in South Vietnam to convince the bulk of the population that they should give allegiance to or actually work for the Saigon regime (military or elected). Second, the Viet Cong are a deeply entrenched force in the society of South Vietnam. The interaction of these two facts—that the Saigon regime is irrelevant to the needs of the population and that the Viet Cong are still a deeply rooted power in the South—explains the continuance of strength by the Viet Cong. The policy of escalation can never come to grips with the root problem, which is the unregenerate, unreformed, ineffective character of the Saigon regime.

As Secretary McNamara observed in his Montreal speech of May 16, 1967, "There is an irrefutable relationship between violence and economic backwardness" in underdeveloped countries. He draws the conclusion that "In modernizing society, security means development." It is in this, not a military role, that we can help provide security. "We have no charter to rescue floundering regimes who have brought violence on themselves by deliberately refusing to meet the legitimate aspirations of their citizenry." This, military hardware cannot supply.[6]

Obviously, Saigon meets the definition of a "floundering regime" whose ills cannot be cured by our military action, by our policy of escalation. As R. W. Apple of *The New York Times* concluded in August 1967, "If the North Vietnamese and American troops were magically whisked away, the South Vietnamese regime would almost certainly crumble within months, so little have the root problems been touched."[7]

That the Saigon regime, despite optimistic public relations reports issued by the administration, is not improving the lives of the people of South Vietnam was directly confirmed by the South Vietnamese themselves in the CBS public opinion poll at the beginning of 1967. To the question, "Do you think that your life is better or worse than it was a year ago?" 75 per cent responded that their lives either were worse or had not improved. Even this figure is a considerable underestimate of the failure of the Saigon regime to meet the "legitimate aspirations of their citizenry," since the urban and middle classes were admittedly overrepresented among those interviewed and only 22 per cent of those questioned in this predominantly agricultural nation were farmers. Moreover, the poll did not reach a fair proportion of the refugee population.[8]

As usual, the administration is optimistic in its announced expectations that the "new" elected government of President Thieu will be able to carry out all of the reforms needed to win the hearts and minds of the people. To me, this is pure nonsense. Are we to believe that Thieu and Ky have been hiding their reformism during the past two years they were in power, only to miraculously implement now what they were then able but unwilling to do? The Saigon regimes have never given the South Vietnamese an ideal worth fighting and dying to preserve. Nor have they been able to demonstrate the strength, power, or effectiveness that can convince their enemies to give up the struggle.

How can we extricate ourselves from Vietnam? Secretary Rusk continues to tell us that the problem lies with the "other side," that the administration is for "peace" but that the "other side" is not, that the administration is for "negotiations" but that Hanoi is not. This reiterated position has misled and deluded the American people about the nature of the real conflict in Vietnam and consequently about the way to find a settlement to that conflict.

The terms "peace" and "negotiations" as currently employed by the administration have all of the clarity and sacredness of the term "motherhood." Obviously, the administration is for it, and our enemies on the other side are against it.

What is the real meaning of the terms "peace" and "negotiations"? Is Secretary Rusk's view accurate, is he capable of seeing reality as it really is? In the fall of 1964, as we now know, the N.L.F. was quite willing to "negotiate" for "peace," i.e., they were willing to negotiate (in effect) the surrender to them of the South Vietnamese government forces so near collapse. Saigon and its U.S. "advisors" did not choose to negotiate under those circumstances. With Saigon in an improved position, President Johnson's letter to Ho Chi Minh in February 1967 revealed that the administration then was willing to "negotiate" (in effect) the surrender of the Viet Cong-North Vietnamese forces. Ho replied, after bombing of the North was resumed, that *he* did not choose to negotiate under those circumstances.

Assertions about who is for peace and who is for negotiations obscure the basic reality that *there is a struggle being waged over who should govern South Vietnam.* The administration believes, as a part of its theory of aggression, that only Saigon is the legitimate representative of the people of South Vietnam. Our adversaries, as the foundation of their belief in the Geneva Agreements of 1954 and their faith in the Viet Cong infrastructure show, believe that Saigon is not the legitimate representative of the people of South Vietnam. If we are to be honest, we must admit that the term "negotiations" means mutual concessions and joint accommodation, not victory. If one side forces the other to give up its objectives by the use of military force, the result is not negotiation but surrender.

The concept of negotiations can have meaning only in the context of mutual concessions. Until both sides are ready to undertake mutual concessions there can be no meaningful negotiations. Until that time arrives, statements by the administration about which side is for negotiations only serve to obscure the fundamental fact that the struggle being waged is really over who has the right to rule South Vietnam.

The public relations position of the administration on negotiations hides the basis for achieving a settlement of the war in Vietnam. Every indicator tells us that the root problems there cannot be solved by massive application of American military force. It is abundantly clear that the war has been, and remains, in an indecisive stage of stalemate as a result.

I believe that both sides have been intransigent as far as moving the stalemate from the battlefield into a conference of meaningful negotiations. Contrary to the administration, I do not believe that either

Saigon or the N.L.F. has ever demonstrated that it is really interested in the welfare of the people of Vietnam. The only conclusion we can reach is that it is logically impossible for us to impose the Saigon regime on the Vietnamese populace. Moreover, I want to make it absolutely clear that I believe that morally we *should not* try to impose the Saigon regime on the Vietnamese populace. Rather, as the stronger power, as the power which has traditionally represented what is just and what is right, we must take the initiative for moving the stalemated war from the battlefield to the conference table. We must not match the intransigence of our adversaries with an intransigence of our own.

In order to have a viable policy for settlement we must come to grips with the fact that the only government that could possibly be representative of all the Vietnamese people would be a coalition government. The administration must decide to accept this ultimate solution and give up its futile, costly, and dangerous attempt to prop up a pseudo-civilian military Saigon regime for the people of South Vietnam. This is the first decision that the administration must make to establish the basis for a settlement of the war in Vietnam.

What else should be done to achieve a settlement?

During the United Nations session which opened in September 1967 a steady stream of America's allies and nonaligned countries called for a halt in the bombing of the North. Many of these diplomats confirmed that they had every reason to believe that negotiations would begin within three to four weeks after a halt in the bombing. Many prominent figures in the United States, both Democrats and Republicans, have also called for a halt in the bombing, as I have done repeatedly. Given these pleas, given the military impotence of the bombing according to the McNamara testimony, given the falling popularity and confidence in the leadership of the President, it is quite possible that there will be another pause in the bombing between the time this book is written and the Presidential election of 1968.

I have given in this book extensive quotations from the testimony of Secretary McNamara that the bombing of North Vietnam cannot reduce significantly the flow of supplies into the South. In additional testimony released on October 10, 1967, the Secretary expressed the doubt that a pause in the bombing would cause an increase in American casualties.

Will such a pause in the bombing, or any of the other suggested tactical moves of de-escalation, provide the basis for a settlement of the war in Vietnam? As much as we all want to see an end to bloodshed in that ill-fated country, I do not believe there is any one dramatic action, any panacea, that will provide an easy way out of the morass. Halting the bombing of the North may set the stage for talks, but it has nothing to do with deciding to work for reconciliation of the significant differences and divisions within the South. One dramatic act of de-escalation after many acts of escalation will not provide a way to meaningful negotiations.

On the other hand, what can lead toward a settlement that will protect the best interests and preserve the traditional values of the United States? I have discussed in this book the social and political realities of Vietnam, pointing out the fallacies in the policy of escalation which prevent that policy from being successful. Only a *whole* policy, based upon the true realities and upon recognition of the errors of the policy of escalation, can serve to lead America out of the war in Vietnam. Such a settlement of the Vietnam war will, as I have indicated in this book, protect the vital interests and preserve the honored values of the United States.

Perhaps the most important, and primary, consideration is the necessity to understand that the initiative lies with *our* side. For the reasons I have mentioned we can abandon the policy of escalation, we can abandon the policy of bombing North Vietnam, and most importantly we can abandon the attempt to impose the Saigon regime upon the people of South Vietnam. When the administration makes these decisions we will be in a position to discuss mutual concessions that will offer the prospect of meaningful negotiations.

I do not underestimate the difficulties of persuading our adversaries to join us in making mutual concessions; there is no ironclad assurance that the N.L.F. and Hanoi are ready to join us in this process. But the significant consideration is that *we* have the opportunity to take the initiative, to establish an affirmative position. Once this decision has been taken by the administration, third parties are both able and willing to bring pressure on the N.L.F. and Hanoi to participate in meaningful negotiations in order to bring an end to the killing in Vietnam.

The administration's fixation about who is for peace and negotiations or how to find the "key" to negotiations, in Secretary Rusk's phrase, pushes far into the background the two crucial factors that there is a struggle over who is to represent the people of South Vietnam and that the policy of escalation only exacerbates but cannot provide a solution to that problem. We must reject the administration's approach about who is for negotiations as leading the American public away from the essential issues in Vietnam.

I have refrained from outlining specific details here on mechanisms for, or proposed content of, a settlement of the American crisis in Vietnam. My purpose has not been to spell out the specifics, the details, the procedural steps that must be taken to achieve resolution of the problems confronting us.

The position I have outlined above provides the basis for attaining a settlement of the American crisis in Vietnam. My primary area of responsibility does not extend into these matters of detail, of *how* to carry out a policy, of precisely which steps to take and when. The role of a United States Senator, or any concerned citizen outside of the government, is not necessarily to list the methods and the steps which the diplomats should follow. But we must know the facts, then apply to them the *principles* which America stands for in order to derive a broad policy true to these principles.

Among the principles which I believe correct are the principle of resisting aggression; of not becoming involved in a land war in Asia; of not supporting bankrupt regimes; of honoring American commitments to the international rule of law. When I look at what is going on in Vietnam I am aware that we are not upholding or being true to any of these principles.

The aim of this book has been to show why we must bring an end to the policy of escalation and why we must bring an end to the attempt to shore up a bankrupt and ineffective regime. Rather than describe the details of how to carry out a policy, I believe that I must identify the basic direction we must follow and the basic decisions we must make in order to establish the policy that protects America's vital interests and preserves America's revered values. After these pivotal decisions have been made, then the functionaries can work on the details of how best to implement these decisions. At this particular time, the problem before us is not how to carry out a policy but to make the fundamental decisions regarding what we want America to do and to stand for.

Secretary Rusk has stated that "The debate in which we are now involved is essentially a debate about detail—this or that military move, this or that diplomatic step, this or that formulation."[9] This debate is not about *details* but about the basic *principles* of American national purpose. To me, the debate is not about *how* to do something but about *what* we want America to do with her power. When Secretary Rusk reveals how poorly he understands his fellow Americans, he demonstrates again how blind he is to the realities of the world. For we are not debating over details but over life and death for thousands of human beings. We are not debating over details but over the whole conception of the noble national purpose which America ought to hold forth for the people of the world.

I believe that we have no mandate to bulwark bankrupt regimes against the fruits of their own folly. I believe that the people of the world will be better served by the virtues of the American example than by the employment of American military power. I believe that we cannot violate the pledges for the peaceful settlement of international disputes contained in the United Nations Charter and then demand that others live according to that international "rule by law."

The gracious bounty of America deserves to be employed in building a better way of life for our people at home and for all of the peoples of the world. We will not be able to fulfill the promise of American life while America's precious human and material resources are being wasted in a land war in Vietnam. Other well-meaning American leaders have told us before that winning just this *one* war will make the world safe for freedom and democracy. We know that war and killing cannot help us to realize our constructive goals. We must work toward these ends slowly and painfully. We know that we will be able to achieve the lofty promise of America only in peace.

Notes

Introduction

1. Gallup poll, *The New York Times,* October 9, 1967.

2. Louis Harris, "The Harris Survey: Public Confidence in President Plunges to All-Time Low of 23%," *Washington Post,* November 13, 1967. The exact question asked was, "If you had to choose one course the U.S. should follow in Vietnam, which one would you choose?" The same question in July showed the same number (21%) in favor of "win total military victory," but those for "fight on to get negotiated peace" were then twice as numerous (51% in July, 26% in late October). From July's 24% favoring "get out as quickly as possible" the number had increased to 44%. As Mr. Harris interpreted the figures, "This means that 65% of Americans want a change in our Vietnam policy."

3. Lyndon B. Johnson, *My Hope for America* (New York: 1964), pp. 65–66.

4. "Goldwater Sides with Johnson on Strategy of Vietnam War," *The New York Times,* April 10, 1967.

5. David S. Broder, "Reagan Wins Two Audiences in Nebraska," *Washington Post,* June 25, 1967, p. A23.

6. Department of State Publication 2353, *Charter of the United Nations.*

7. Tom Buckley, "Nixon Urges Halt to War Criticism," *The New York Times,* April 15, 1967, p. 2; datelined Saigon.

8. Tom Buckley, "Nixon Indicates He Seeks Stepup in War Effort," *The New York Times,* April 18, 1967, p. 2; datelined Saigon.

9. The first quote ("strangely silent") is from President Johnson, speech text in *The New York Times,* July 25, 1966, p. 4; others in order, Johnson

speech, March 16, 1967, p. 9; Dean Rusk, Chicago speech, July 6, 1967; Johnson speech, March 16, 1967; June 28, 1967, p. 24; all *ibid.*

10. Figure used by Hanson Baldwin, military editor, *The New York Times*, February 21, 1965.

11. John F. Kennedy, *Public Papers of the Presidents, 1963* (Washington: Government Printing Office), p. 460.

12. J. William Fulbright, *The Arrogance of Power* (New York: 1966), p. 22.

Chapter I

1. James Reston, "The Yen to 'Do Something,' " *The New York Times*, January 5, 1966, p. 30.

2. "Transcript of President's Speech to Junior Chamber of Commerce in Baltimore," *The New York Times*, June 28, 1967, p. 24.

3. Frank N. Trager, "American Foreign Policy in Southeast Asia," in *Studies on Asia, 1965*, R. K. Sakai, ed. (Lincoln: University of Nebraska, 1965), p. 28. Originally presented as a paper before the 13th annual meeting of the Midwestern Conference on Asian Affairs, held at the University of Southern Illinois, October 1964.

4. Marvin E. Gettleman, ed., *Viet Nam: History, Documents and Opinions on a Major World Crisis* (New York: Fawcett, 1965), pp. 19–20; as reprinted from Roy Jumper and Marjorie Normand, "Vietnam," in *Government and Politics of Southeast Asia,* edited by George McT. Kahin (Ithaca, N.Y., 1964).

5. *Ibid.*, p. 26.

6. *Ibid.*, p. 37; from Harold Isaacs, *No Peace for Asia* (New York: Macmillan, 1947).

7. Malcolm Salmon, *Focus on Indo-China* (Hanoi: Foreign Languages Publishing House, 1962), p. 60.

8. Allen B. Cole, ed., *Conflict in Indo-China and International Repercussions: A Documentary History, 1945–1955* (Ithaca, N.Y.: Cornell University Press, 1956), p. xx.

9. Salmon, *op. cit.*, p. 74. The "popular front" is a well-tried Communist technique.

10. Cole, *Documentary History*, pp. 17–18.

11. *Ibid.*, p. 21.

12. Ellen J. Hammer, *The Struggle for Indochina* (Palo Alto, Calif.: Stanford University Press, 1954), p. 108.

13. Jean-Michel Hertrich, *Doc Lap!* (Paris, 1946), p. 49; quoted by Hammer, p. 116.

14. Hammer, *loc. cit.*

15. *Journal of the Royal Central Asian Society* (London), July–October, 1953, p. 213.

16. Harold Isaacs, *No Peace for Asia;* in Gettleman, *op. cit.*, p. 45.

17. Cole, *Documentary History*, pp. 40–42, gives full text of both the Agreement and the Military Annex.

18. Some accounts charge bombing also. For two versions, see Bernard Fall, *The Two Viet-Nams* (New York: Praeger, 1963), p. 76, and Hammer, *op. cit.*, pp. 182–83.

19. Hammer, *op. cit.*, pp. 188–89.

Chapter II

1. William C. Bullitt, "The Saddest War," *Life*, December 29, 1947. He does not mention Chinese dangers, of course, because the Nationalists under Chiang Kai-shek had not given way to the Chinese Communists.

2. *The New York Times*, February 4, 1947; cited in Hammer, *op. cit.*, p. 196.

3. *Le Monde*, February 15, 1947; as quoted in Hammer, p. 196.

4. *Supra*, p. 19. See Chapter I, footnote 17.

5. Hammer, *The Struggle for Indochina*, p. 204.

6. *Ibid.*

7. *Ibid.*, p. 207.

8. *L'Express*, December 19, 1953; *ibid.*, p. 212 fn.

9. Hammer, *op. cit.*, p. 213.

10. Cole, *Documentary History*, p. 70.

11. During this period Bao Dai, who achieved an international reputation as a "playboy," was out of the country.

12. Robert Shaplen, *The Lost Revolution* (rev. ed.; New York: 1966), p. 64.

13. *Ibid.*, p. 87. The economic aid mission was a forerunner of the present AID operation.

14. Opinion Research Corporation, *The People of Vietnam: How They Feel About the War* (Princeton: March 1967), p. 37.

15. Theodore Draper, *Abuse of Power* (New York: 1967), p. 29.

16. Shaplen, *op. cit.*, p. 26.

17. Department of State *Bulletin*, May 22, 1950, p. 821; quoted in Gettleman, *Viet Nam: History, Documents and Opinions*, p. 89. Italics added.

18. Robert Scheer, *How the United States Got Involved in Vietnam* (Santa Barbara, Calif.: Center for the Study of Democratic Institutions, 1965), p. 10.

19. Shaplen, *op. cit.*, p. 66.

20. Draper, *op. cit.*, p. 29.

21. Ellen J. Hammer, "Indochina," in Lawrence K. Rosinger and Associates, *The State of Asia: A Contemporary Survey* (New York: Knopf, 1951); as reprinted in Gettleman, *op cit.*, p. 85.

22. From figures published in *Le Monde*, July 21, 1954; Cole, *Documentary History*, p. 259.

23. *Journal Officiel* of the French National Assembly; Hammer, *The Struggle for Indochina*, p. 313 fn.
24. Figures cited appear with a detailed breakdown in Cole, *Documentary History*, in tables on pp. 260–61.
25. Shaplen, *op. cit.*, p. 89.
26. *Ibid.*, p. 56.
27. Some estimates run as high as 85 per cent, and Dien Bien Phu has been called "a German battle" by some. The casualty figures are found in Cole, *Documentary History*, taken from a USIS report published in 1955 by our embassy in Paris, drawn from French sources.
28. National Council of Churches *Information Service*, February 26, 1966.
29. The Presidential Seal appears on this publication and it was apparently issued by the White House rather than the State Department. President Johnson says in the Foreword: "I have therefore directed that this report to the American people be compiled and widely distributed."
30. *Congressional Record*, June 15, 1965, p. 13193.
31. Dennis Warner, *The Last Confucian* (Penguin Books, 1964), p. 236.

Chapter III

1. Department of State *Bulletin*, November 15, 1954, pp. 735–36. Italics added.
2. Lester A. Sobel, ed., *South Vietnam: U. S.–Communist Confrontation in Southeast Asia 1961–1965* (New York: Facts on File, 1966), p. 207.
3. Chester Bowles, "Topics: Who Owns the Land?", *The New York Times*, July 22, 1967.
4. Text of all three documents appears in Gettleman, *op. cit.*, pp. 137–59.
5. Committee on Foreign Relations, U.S. Senate, *Hearings*, 89th Congress, 2nd Session, "Supplemental Foreign Assistance, Fiscal Year 1966—Vietnam," p. 148.
6. Gettleman, *Viet Nam: History, Documents and Opinions*, p. 172.
7. Dwight D. Eisenhower, *Mandate for Change* (Garden City, N.Y.: Doubleday, 1963), p. 372.
8. Department of State *Bulletin*, April 4, 1966, p. 530.
9. Senate speech, *Congressional Record*, April 9, 1965, p. 7664. In the order given, the preceding phrases are from Robert Scigliano, *South Vietnam: Nation Under Stress* (Boston: Houghton Mifflin, 1963), p. 134; George McT. Kahin and John W. Lewis, *op. cit.*, p. 31; and Richard N. Goodwin, *Triumph or Tragedy: Reflections on Vietnam* (New York: Random House, 1966), p. 25.
10. *Hearings*, p. 341.
11. Scigliano, *op. cit.*, 134.
12. *Congressional Record*, February 1, 1955, p. 1051.
13. Department of State *Bulletin*, January 1, 1962, p. 14.

14. "The President's Remarks to Troops and Speech to Korean National Assembly," *The New York Times*, November 2, 1966, p. 16, col. 3. Quotation is from the "Talk to American and Korean Servicemen at Camp Stanley, South Korea."
15. Arthur M. Schlesinger, Jr., *A Thousand Days: John F. Kennedy in the White House* (Boston: 1965), p. 547.
16. Television interview with Walter Cronkite (CBS), September 2, 1963; Senate Committee on Foreign Relations, *Background Information Relating to Southeast Asia and Vietnam* (2nd rev. ed.), March 1966, p. 107.
17. Department of State, *Viet Nam: The Struggle for Freedom* (1964), p. 21.
18. Gettleman, *op. cit.*, p. 205.
19. Philippe Devillers, "The Struggle for Unification of Vietnam," *China Quarterly* (London), January–March, 1962; reprinted in Gettleman, *op. cit.*, p. 223.
20. *Ibid.*
21. *Ibid.*, p. 224.
22. Wesley Fishel, "Vietnam's Democratic One-Man Rule," *The New Leader*, November 2, 1959, pp. 10–13.
23. Wesley R. Fishel, "Vietnam: Is Victory Possible?" in Foreign Policy Association *Headline Series*, February 1964, p. 16, as cited in Gettleman, *op. cit.*, p. 191. It was Fishel, who first met Diem in Japan in 1950, who arranged to bring him to the United States where his three-year stay helped gain him U.S. support in high places.

Chapter IV

1. *Congressional Record*, February 21, 1966, p. 3414.
2. Tom Buckley, "Foe's Loss at 359 in Queson Battle," *The New York Times*, January 5, 1968; also Buckley, "U.S. Dead at 543 in Week, a Record," *ibid.*, February 23, 1968.
3. Douglas Pike, *Viet Cong* (Cambridge, Mass.: M.I.T. Press, 1966), p. 73.
4. Quoted in Scheer, *How the United States Got Involved in Vietnam*, p. 53.
5. David Halberstam, *The Making of a Quagmire* (New York: Random House, 1965), p. 69.
6. John Mecklin, *Mission in Torment* (Garden City, N.Y.: Doubleday, 1965), pp. 31–32.
7. Schlesinger, *A Thousand Days*, p. 545.
8. The Military Assistance Advisory Group (MAAG) had been subordinated to a newly established Military Assistance Command, Vietnam (MACV), headed by newly promoted four-star General Paul D. Harkins, formerly deputy commander-in-chief for the Pacific.
9. Lester Sobel, ed., *South Vietnam: U.S.–Communist Confrontation in Southeast Asia, 1961–65* (New York: Facts on File, 1966), p. 58. Much

of the escalation chronology presented in this chapter is based on this concise but comprehensive compendium by the publishers of *Facts on File.*

10. *Viet Nam and Southeast Asia*, Senate Committee on Foreign Relations, February 25, 1963, p. 5.

11. *The Vietnam Conflict: The Substance and the Shadow*, Senate Committee on Foreign Relations, January 6, 1966, p. 3. The 1963 report also appears as an appendix in this document.

12. Arthur M. Schlesinger, Jr., "A Middle Way Out of Vietnam," *The New York Times*, September 18, 1966.

13. Herman Kahn, *On Escalation: Metaphors and Scenarios* (Hudson Institute, Harmon, N.Y., 1965), p. 7.

14. Other instances as well as these are discussed in my Senate speech of June 30, 1966, widely circulated as a reprint under the title "Our Policy of Escalation." *Congressional Record*, June 30, 1966, p. 14197–204.

15. *Congressional Record*, August 6, 1964, p. 18425.

16. *Le Monde*, August 5, 1964; quoted in Schurmann, Scott and Zelnik, *The Politics of Escalation in Vietnam*, p. 41.

17. Full text appeared in *The New York Times*, August 4, 1964; reprinted in *Congressional Record*, August 7, 1964, p. 18459. "Top secret" Defense Department materials released by Senator Morse, according to the *Washington Post*, February 23, 1968, "have reportedly convinced not only Morse but a majority of the Senate Foreign Relations Committee that the administration—by accident or design—misled both Congress and the American public on the events that triggered the first bombing on August 4, 1964."

A "log of events" published in the same issue showed that neither destroyer ever visually sighted the PT boats, but fired at three-mile range by radar direction at 9:39 P.M. under a "very dark, moonless, overcast sky." At 2:50 A.M., after numerous messages reporting the "battle"—including a count of as many as 22 torpedoes fired by the unseen enemy—the *Maddox*, answering an evaluation request by the task group commander, said ". . . entire action leaves many doubts . . ." and suggested thorough air reconnaissance at daylight.

At 5:30 A.M. the Commander in Chief, Pacific (CINCPAC), asked confirmation "absolutely" of attack and sinking of PT boats, including "directly supporting evidence." The *Maddox* reply, at 6 A.M., was that the first boat "probably fired a torpedo which was heard but not seen. All subsequent torpedo reports are doubtful in that it is suspected that the sonar man was hearing the ship's own propeller beat."

At that time it was 6 P.M. in Washington. An hour and a half earlier the President had already approved the reprisal strike, although the 2:50 *Maddox* message was in hand and there were doubts "beginning to arise" as a result. At 6:30 P.M. (Washington time) the reprisal order went from the Pentagon to CINCPAC, which again asked the *Maddox* for "urgent confirmation," which neither destroyer could supply.

The *Maddox'* grave doubts of its own torpedo reports, given to CINCPAC four hours earlier—before the Pentagon order—reached Washington via cable at 10:59 P.M.; it was 11:37 that the President went on television to denounce North Vietnam's "open aggression on the high seas" and to report our retaliatory strike, by then in progress.

See Richard Harwood, "Morse Releases Secret Material" and Walter Pincus, "Log of Events Before Bombing of North Vietnam by U.S. in 1964," both subheads to the single caption "Tonkin: The Mounting Debate," *Washington Post*, February 23, 1968, p. A1; also p. A14, Chalmers M. Roberts, "Morse and McNamara Contentions on Tonkin Gulf Events." Material in this footnote was unavailable when the account in Chapter IV was written.

18. *The New York Times*, August 5, 1964; reprinted in *Congressional Record*, same date, p. 18135. Other citations from *New York Herald Tribune*, August 7, 1964, "As Others See the Tonkin Gulf," *Congressional Record*, same date, p. 18469; and Marquis Childs, "Vietnam of 1964 Recalls Korea of 1950," *Washington Post*, August 7, 1964, also *Congressional Record*, same date, p. 18460.

19. I. F. Stone, "International Law and the Tonkin Bay Incidents," *I. F. Stone's Weekly*, August 24, 1964, as reprinted in Marcus G. Raskin and Bernard B. Fall, *The Viet-Nam Reader: Articles and Documents on American Foreign Policy and the Viet-Nam Crisis* (New York: Random House, 1965), p. 309.

20. Text of U.S. resolution is in *The New York Times*, November 26, 1966.

21. Schurmann, Scott and Zelnik, *op. cit.*, p. 46.

22. Charles Roberts, *LBJ's Inner Circle* (New York: Dell, 1965), pp. 20–21.

23. *The New York Times*, February 8, 1965.

24. Schurmann, Scott and Zelnik, *op. cit.*, p. 54.

25. Charles E. Osgood, *Perspective in Foreign Policy* (Palo Alto, Calif.: Pacific Books, 1965), p. 16.

26. Waverley Root, "Visitor to Hanoi Tells of War Toll There," *Washington Post*, November 27, 1966, p. A29.

27. Osgood, *op. cit.*, p. 23.

Chapter V

1. Morley Safer, "Television Covers the War," *Dateline 1966* (Overseas Press Club of America, New York); reprinted in *Congressional Record*, May 12, 1966, p. 9978.

2. Henry J. Taylor, "Viet War Will Be Lost in Washington," *Wilmington* (Delaware) *Morning News*, May 7, 1966; *Congressional Record*, May 10, 1966, p. 9656.

3. Walter Trohan, "Sylvester's At It Again," reprinted from *Chicago Tribune* in *Human Events*, July 23, 1966. Sylvester gave his own version and reaffirmed his basic position in an article, "The Government Has the Right to Lie," in the *Saturday Evening Post*, November 18, 1967. He resigned from the Defense Department post on February 3, 1967 after six years under three presidents.

4. Eric Sevareid, "The Final Troubled Hours of Adlai Stevenson," *Look*, November 30, 1965.

5. Thomas J. Hamilton, "Thant Asks Vietnam Talks . . . ," *The New York Times*, February 25, 1965.

6. Murrey Marder, "Our Crumbling Credibility," *The Progressive*, August 1966.

7. *The New York Times*, December 29, 1965, p. 2. Italics added.

8. Department of State Publication 8050, "Viet-Nam: The 38th Day," p. 4.

9. "Periscope," *Newsweek*, December 5, 1966.

10. John W. Finney, "Rusk Lists 28 Bids on Vietnam Peace Spurned by Hanoi," *The New York Times*, May 2, 1967.

11. *The New York Times*, March 22, 1967.

12. "Text of Goldberg's Address on Vietnam, Africa and Space," *The New York Times*, September 23, 1966.

13. Wilfred Burchett, "Red Writer Gives Hanoi's Views," *Washington Post*, February 8, 1967.

14. Lee Lockwood, "Salisbury's Stake," *New York Review of Books*, August 3, 1967.

15. "Text of Johnson's Letter to Ho Chi Minh and the North Vietnamese Reply," *The New York Times*, March 22, 1967.

16. Interview on "Meet the Press" (NBC), April 4, 1965.

17. Department of State *Bulletin*, April 11, 1966, p. 569.

18. "Lodge Asks Army Role in New Regime," *The New York Times*, April 26, 1967.

Chapter VI

1. Department of State Publication 7839, *Aggression From the North: The Record of North Viet-Nam's Campaign To Conquer South Viet-Nam*, February, 1965, p. 29.

2. *Ibid.*

3. *Ibid.*, p. 1.

4. Opinion Research Corporation, *The People of South Vietnam* (mimeographed; Princeton: 1965).

5. Raskin and Fall, *Viet-Nam Reader*, p. 118.

6. Bernard Fall, "Vietnam: The New Korea," *Current History*, February 1966.

7. John Alden, *American Revolution* (New York: 1954), p. 244.

8. Samuel Bemis, *Diplomacy of the American Revolution* (Bloomington, Indiana: Indiana University Press, 1957), p. 255.

9. Department of State Publication 7308, December 1961.

10. I. F. Stone, "A Reply to the White Paper," *I. F. Stone's Weekly*, March 8, 1965; also reprinted in Gettleman, *Viet Nam: History, Documents and*

Opinions, pp. 317–23; and Raskin and Fall, *The Viet-Nam Reader,* pp. 155–62.

11. Mike Mansfield, "Viet-Nam and China," address given at Yeshiva University, New York, June 16, 1966.

12. Department of State *Bulletin,* May 17, 1965.

13. *The New York Times,* February 28, 1965.

14. Walter Rostow, address given June 1961; reprinted in Raskin and Fall, *Viet-Nam Reader,* p. 113.

15. "Transcript of Secretary Rusk's News Conference," *The New York Times,* October 13, 1967, p. 14.

16. Robert McNamara, address given March 1964; reprinted in Raskin and Fall, *op. cit.,* pp. 194–204.

17. *Ibid.*

18. Douglas Pike, *Viet Cong* (M.I.T. Press: 1966), p. 325. Pike's use of the past tense is due to the significant distinction he makes between the period up to late 1964, when our heavy escalation and the corresponding increase of Northern intervention began, and the period since. He writes in the preface (p. ix): "The struggle in Vietnam was in fact two wars, one following the other. The first began in 1960, or possibly as early as 1958, and ended in late 1964 or early 1965. After that time, Vietnam was the arena of a new war, with new actors, new ground rules, new tactics and strategy, new definitions of victory and defeat. This book is about the first war, which, if the two-wars contention is accepted, does then have a beginning, middle, and end (which explains why the book is written in past tense)."

19. *The New York Times,* October 13, 1967.

20. Full text of the speech, together with a lengthy colloquy which followed between Senator Kennedy and Senators Knowland, Symington, Jackson and others, may be found in the *Congressional Record,* April 6, 1954, pp. 4672–81.

21. Marvin L. Stone, "Is U.S. Trapped in a 'Hopeless War'?", *U.S. News and World Report,* December 5, 1966, p. 45.

22. R. W. Apple, Jr., "Saigon's Army: A U.S. Challenge," *New York Times,* December 12, 1966, p. 10, col. 4.

23. Ward Just, "Peasants Cater Troops' Lunch," *Washington Post,* November 28, 1966.

24. Marvin Stone, *op. cit.,* p. 49.

25. Apple, *op. cit.* (both quotes).

26. Stone, *op. cit.,* p. 44.

27. R. W. Apple, Jr., "U.S. Study Calls a Night Army Essential for Victory in Vietnam," *The New York Times,* August 6, 1967.

28. *Ibid.*

29. Ward Just, "This War May Be Unwinnable," *Washington Post,* June 4, 1967.

30. Sir Robert Thompson, "A Briton on U.S. in Vietnam," *The New York Times,* September 10, 1967, p. E13.

31. Neil Sheehan, "Not a Dove, But No Longer a Hawk," *The New York Times Magazine,* October 9, 1966.

32. Editorial, "The Most Powerful Bomb," *The New York Times,* August 31, 1967.

Chapter VII

1. "Why Not Say So?" *The New York Times,* December 16, 1966.

2. Harrison E. Salisbury, "Visitor to Hanoi Inspects Damage Attributed to American Raids," "Raids Leave Blocks Razed, Fail to Cut Lines to Hanoi," *The New York Times,* December 26 and 27, 1966.

3. Neil Sheehan, "U.S. Concedes That Bombs Hit Civilian Areas in North Vietnam," *The New York Times,* December 27, 1966.

4. Minoru Omori, "Report from Hanoi," *Mainichi,* as reprinted in *Viet-Report,* November–December 1965.

5. Albert Axlebank, "Japan—The Two Reischauers," *New Republic,* November 13, 1965.

6. The United States Strategic Bombing Survey *Summary Report* (September 30, 1945), p. 1.

7. Alan Barth, "Strategic Bombing—An Autopsy," *The Nation,* November 24, 1945.

8. Ward Just, "Intensified Bombing Shaken Off by Hanoi," *Washington Post,* December 29, 1966.

9. U.S. Senate Committee on Armed Services, Hearings before the Preparedness Investigating Subcommittee January 26, March 9, 15, and 17, 1966, *Status of Ammunition and Air Munitions,* p. 129.

10. Editorial, "Bombs in Hanoi's Center," *The New York Times,* August 24, 1967.

11. *The New York Times,* August 29, 1967. Mr. Schoenbrunn is currently a professor at Columbia University.

12. "Bombing Hanoi," *Washington Post,* December 29, 1966.

13. U.S. Strategic Bombing Survey *Report,* p. 3.

14. Hanson W. Baldwin, "Bombing of the North," *The New York Times,* September 28, 1966.

15. "Another Pilot's Report from Vietnam," *Aviation Week and Space Technology,* October 24, 1966.

16. "Pilot Report from Vietnam," *ibid.,* September 19, 1966.

17. As cited above, fn. 8. The subhead is, "How Many Bridges Were There?"

18. *Op. cit.*

19. "Red Visits North Viet Nam: Hanoi Chiefs Called Sure of Victory," *Washington Star,* June 5, 1966. Harrison Salisbury six months later devoted an entire dispatch to the use of bicycles in North Vietnam, to-

gether with a two-column picture of such "freight bicycles." Harrison E. Salisbury, "North Vietnam Runs on Bicycles," *The New York Times,* January 7, 1967.

20. Matthew B. Ridgway, "Pull-out, All-out, or Stand Fast in Vietnam?" *Look,* April 5, 1966, p. 84.

21. *The New York Times,* December 10, 1965, p. 12.

22. *The New York Times,* August 29, 1967.

23. Neil Sheehan, "Hanoi Bolstering Air Raid Defenses," *The New York Times,* September 28, 1966.

24. Richard Dudman, "Intelligence Agencies' Study Calls Bombing of N. Vietnam a Political, Military Failure," *St. Louis Post-Dispatch,* December 24, 1966.

25. Editorial, "Stalemate Through Air Power," August 26, 1967.

26. U.S. Senate Preparedness Investigating Subcommittee Hearings, *Air War Against North Vietnam,* Part IV, August 25, 1967, pp. 276–281.

27. George C. Wilson, "Johnson Seen Yielding to Pressure in Bombing of N. Vietnamese Port," *Washington Post,* September 12, 1967.

Chapter VIII

1. Stanley Karnow, " 'Mr. Nguyen,' Saigon Employe, Chuckles Over Curbs on Graft," *Washington Post,* February 24, 1966.

2. "New Viet Face: Pep Talks and Candy," *New York Herald Tribune,* February 3, 1964.

3. Conversation in my office, December 1966. Near the end of 1967 it was reported that Mme. Nhu had purchased a sizeable Paris hotel—for cash.

4. Associated Press, "CBS Reports Ky Gets $15,000 a Week Racing Payoff, Called 'Charity' Fund," *Washington Post,* July 29, 1966.

5. "A Dissenting Voice from Vietnam," *Congressional Record,* March 4, 1966, pp. 4727–28.

6. As told to a member of my staff by the returned Air Force officer, who is his brother-in-law.

7. House of Representatives Committee on Government Operations, "An Investigation of the U.S. Economic and Military Assistance Programs in Vietnam" (House Report No. 2257, 89th Congress, 2d Session), October 1966. This is the so-called "Moss report" of the Foreign Operations and Government Information Subcommittee, whose chairman is Congressman John E. Moss of California. The quotation is from p. 25.

8. The GVN budget announced for 1967 is 75 billion piasters, or about $630,000,000; U.S. economic aid for fiscal 1967 is expected to total $681,000. Comparative figures for 1966 and 1967 are:

	1966	1967
GVN budget	55 billion P.	75 billion P. ($630,000,000)
U.S. aid	$727,500,000	$681,000,000

The Government of Vietnam operates on a calendar year basis. Because the piaster was devalued in June 1966 from an official rate of 60 to the dollar to 118 to the dollar, the 1966 dollar equivalent has been omitted. U.S. figures are based on actual costs for Fiscal Year 1966 (July 1, 1965–June 30, 1966) and projected costs for FY 1967 as supplied by the Agency for International Development (AID) in January 1967. U.S. economic aid to South Vietnam by major categories breaks down as follows (millions omitted):

	FY 1966	FY 1967
Technical assistance	$191	$300
Commercial Imports Program	398	230
Agricultural commodities	138.5	151

9. International Bank for Reconstruction and Development, *World Bank Atlas of Per Capita Product and Population*, September 1966.

10. Eric Wentworth, "AID Reports on Losses in Vietnam," *Washington Post*, January 10, 1967.

11. "Moss report," as cited above, fn. 7, p. 17.

12. Gerry Pratt, "Making the Dollar: War-Fueled Inflation Runs Wild in Saigon," Portland *Oregonian*, February 21, 1966; *Congressional Record*, February 28, 1966, p. 4136.

13. Moss report, p. 35: "*Unofficial* losses through covert transactions . . . undoubtedly account for additional losses of foreign exchange and should be of the greatest concern to the United States in view of our present balance-of-payments difficulties."

14. Moss report, p. 17.

15. Charles Bailey, "Fear Reds Got U.S. Explosive," *Des Moines Register*, May 14, 1966; *Congressional Record*, June 9, 1966, p. 12145. See also William C. Selover, "Congressmen See U.S. Aid Dollars Straying in Vietnam," *Christian Science Monitor*, June 8, 1966; *Congressional Record*, June 14, 1966, pp. 12519–20.

16. "Another Enemy in Vietnam War—Corruption," *U.S. News and World Report*, February 14, 1966.

17. Charles Bailey, "Team Seeks to End Viet Misuse," *Des Moines Register*, May 10, 1966; *Congressional Record*, June 9, 1966, p. 12144.

18. Pratt (see 12 above).

19. Moss report, p. 27.

20. See 16 above.

21. Pratt, as cited.

22. Associated Press, "PX Alley: Stubborn Black Market Problem," *The New York Times*, November 16, 1966.

23. Jim G. Lucas, "Americans Gouged in S. Vietnam," *Washington Daily News*, December 19, 1966.

24. Walt Friedenberg, "Vietnamese Resent Execution of Crooked Merchant," *Washington Daily News*, March 15, 1966.

25. Ward Just, "Snipers, VIPs Plague U.S. Pilot Project," *Washington Post*, January 12, 1967.

26. Moss report.
27. *Ibid.*
28. R. W. Apple, Jr., "Circus Time in Saigon," *The New York Times*, January 14, 1967.
29. William S. Gaud, "Management of AID Commodity Programs," January 9, 1967. This is a 30-page "year-end report" to the President from the Administrator of the Agency for International Development, released originally in mimeographed form.
30. For an administration view, see R. W. Komer, *The Other War in Vietnam —A Progress Report* (Washington: Agency for International Development, September 1966). This so-called "Komer report" to the President is filled with statistics of accomplishment and optimistic predictions of further successes to come in every aspect of economic aid. Mr. Komer, then a Special Assistant to the President and now deputy ambassador in Saigon, says in his Letter of Transmittal that it is "mainly a review of accomplishments . . . designed to show how the Government of Vietnam and the U.S. are moving forward on a broad front in an effort to win the 'other war.' " It is not critical.

Chapter IX

1. By February 23, 1968 the total Vietnam death toll was 18,239 Americans —well over half the 33,629 killed in the three-year Korean war. The average weekly death rate to that date in 1968 was 320, double the 1967 average and more than three times the 1966 average of 96. "GI Losses for Week Set Record," *Washington Post*, February 23, 1968.
2. See, for example, David Parks, "Vietnam Diary: The Intimate Story of a Soldier's Ordeal," *Look*, March 19, 1968. The *Look* article is excerpted from the book *G.I. Diary,* scheduled for publication by Harper & Row (New York, 1968).
3. Ward Just, "Poor Security Spoiled Major Campaign in Delta," *Washington Post,* January 20, 1967.
4. Arthur M. Schlesinger, Jr., "A Middle Way Out of Vietnam," *The New York Times Magazine,* September 8, 1966. The same article with slight changes appears in Schlesinger's *The Bitter Heritage: Vietnam and American Democracy, 1941–1966* (Boston: Houghton Mifflin, 1967). He also says in *A Thousand Days: John F. Kennedy in the White House* (Boston, 1965), p. 982: "In the spring of 1963 Alexis Johnson claimed that 30,000 casualties had been inflicted on the guerrillas in 1962—a figure twice as large as the estimated size of the Viet Cong forces at the beginning of the year." The reference, but not the citation, appears as a footnote in Noam Chomsky, "The Responsibility of Intellectuals," *The New York Review,* February 23, 1967.
5. "A Dissenting Voice from Vietnam," *Congressional Record,* March 4, 1966, p. 4727.

6. Donald Duncan, "The Whole Thing Was a Lie!" *Ramparts*, February 1966.

7. The *monthly* average tonnage of bombs dropped on Vietnam exceeded in 1966 the total dropped on Germany—46,000 tons—in all of 1941. See the U.S. Bombing Survey *Summary*, p. 3, as cited in Ch. VII, fn. 6.

8. William Bowen, "The Vietnam War: A Cost Accounting," *Fortune*, April 1966; Hanson W. Baldwin, "New Missions for SAC," *The New York Times*, December 2, 1966; George C. Wilson, "U.S. Spends $332,-000 in War for Each Vietnam Enemy Killed," *Washington Post*, December 18, 1966.

9. Statistics primarily from Bowen, *op. cit.*

10. Bernard B. Fall, "You Can Tell 'Em, Buddy," *New Republic*, January 14, 1967.

11. "What War Is Costing U.S.—A Major Conflict Against a Minor Foe," *U.S. News and World Report*, January 2, 1967.

12. Senate Committee on Armed Services, *Military Procurement Authorizations for Fiscal Year 1967*, p. 744.

13. Hanson W. Baldwin, "Attack on North Is Held Widening," *The New York Times*, December 17, 1966.

14. *Ibid.*

15. William Bowen (see fn. 9 above).

16. George C. Wilson (fn. 8).

17. *U.S. News and World Report*, "Russia: The Enemy in Vietnam?," January 30, 1967, speaks of the war as "costing directly about 30 billion dollars a year." Marquis Childs, "The Cost of War and the Economy," *Washington Post*, September 23, 1966, says, "The war in Vietnam is now costing $2.7 billion a month. Rather than a random figure picked out of the air, this is a careful calculation accepted at the highest level of Government. . . ."

18. The fiscal 1968 budget carries an official estimate of $21.9 billion "clearly attributable" to Vietnam. However, this reflects only direct costs for such items as men and equipment there. For each man on the scene another is required in some other indirect backup relationship, but increased administrative costs are not counted in the $21.9 billion figure. Nor does it allow for the costs of items already on hand. The discrepancy between the listed "direct" costs and the actual total costs are sufficient to bring the latter to the $30 billion figure.

19. As calculated from *Information Please Almanac, 1967* table, "Retail Sales by Kind of Business Group." The figures are Department of Commerce projections for the year as estimated in March 1966.

20. Alan L. Otten, "Nobody Loves a Budget," *Wall Street Journal*, January 25, 1967. "One Administration rundown puts the Great Society increase at $1.9 billion in the coming year, compared with $4.8 billion this year."

21. Richard F. Janssen, "Guidance by Budget," *Wall Street Journal*, January 25, 1967. Janssen then reported anticipated GNP gains of $47.5 billion for 1967, but the actual gain turned out to be only $41.7, to the year's

total of $785 billion. The annual rate for 1967's fourth quarter was $807.3 billion. See *Economic Indicators*, February 1968, p. 2. This is the authoritative publication prepared each month for the Joint Economic Committee by the Council of Economic Advisors.

22. "The bad business of 'war prosperity,'" *Business Week*, August 13, 1966.

23. "Forlorn Hopes," *Time*, May 27, 1966.

24. Hobart Rowen, "Hopes for 'Paper Gold' Could Be War Casualty," *Washington Post*, December 18, 1966. In order to lessen pressure on the dollar and strengthen our gold position in international trade, Congress in 1968 removed the 25 per cent "gold cover" for domestic Federal Reserve notes, freeing the more than $10 billion previously unavailable for international backing of the dollar.

25. Robert S. McNamara, "Security in the Contemporary World," an address to the American Society of Newspaper Editors, Montreal, May 16, 1967.

26. "The Great Vietnam Dilemma," *The Australian*, April 16, 1966; *Congressional Record*, April 18, 1966, p. 7891.

27. Wayne Morse, "The Philippine President and U.S. Policy in Asia," *Congressional Record*, September 19, 1966, p. 22156.

28. "What U.S. Can Expect from Allies in Vietnam," *U.S. News and World Report*, March 14, 1966.

29. "Fighting Tiger for Rent," London *Economist*, February 19, 1966.

30. These countries see no threat in Vietnam, and very little in China. President Ayub Khan of Pakistan has said, "There is no danger to the subcontinent from China provided no uncalled for provocation is aimed against that country." Clayton Fritchey, "Most Nations Oppose U.S. Asia Role," *Washington Star*, June 13, 1966.

31. Office of Public Services, Bureau of Public Affairs, one-page mimeographed sheet, "Other Country Aid to Viet-Nam." Bears notation in lower left "4/35-266BT."

32. *USNWR* (see 28 above). All figures on contributions by other nations are from this source, but since the date is March 1966, the amounts may have altered since.

33. George Gallup, "Voters of Six Nations Differ on Viet Course," Fort Wayne (Ind.) *Journal-Gazette*, November 13, 1966. The question asked was: "Just from what you have heard or read, which of these statements comes closest to the way you, yourself, feel about the war in Viet Nam? A. The U.S. should begin to withdraw its troops. B. The U.S. should carry on its present level of fighting. C. The U.S. should increase the strength of its attacks on North Viet Nam." 25 per cent in Britain, 15 per cent in West Germany, and 19 per cent in France were classed as "No opinion."

34. William Foote Whyte, "Analogies and Images: Thoughtways of Foreign Policy," *The Nation*, May 30, 1966; reprinted in *Congressional Record*, June 7, 1966, p. 11857.

35. Gallup, *ibid.*

36. "The Asahi Poll on Vietnam," *Japan Quarterly*, October–December, 1965. The questions and responses: "Have you read or heard of the bombings of North Vietnam by South Vietnam and American planes?" Yes, 79 per cent; No, 21 per cent. "Do you support or oppose these bombings?" Support, 4 per cent; oppose, 75 per cent; other replies, 4 per cent; no reply, 17 per cent.

37. "Sen. Morton Says Atlantic Summit May Be Necessary to Assure Allies," *Washington Post*, November 1, 1966.

38. *The New York Times*, October 30, 1966, p. 5.

39. Lester Velie, "Our Leaky Pipeline to Vietnam," *Reader's Digest*, December 1966.

40. Clayton Fritchey, "Most Nations Oppose U.S. Asia Role," *Washington Star*, June 13, 1966.

Chapter X

1. William F. Pepper, "The Children of Vietnam," *Ramparts*, January 1967. Dr. Pepper, Director of the Children's Institute for Advanced Study and Research at Mercy College, Dobbs Ferry, New York, and Executive Director of the New Rochelle Commission on Human Rights, spent six weeks in South Vietnam in 1966. His article is accompanied by twenty of his own striking color photographs of Vietnamese children in hospitals and orphanages, some badly burned and otherwise injured, all casualties of the war. His statistics, however, have been called "distorted" and have created much controversy. See 4 below.

2. Martha Gellhorn, *A New Kind of War* (*Manchester Guardian*, 1966), p. 6. This "Guardian Booklet" (*The Manchester Guardian*, 20 East 53rd St., New York, N.Y. 10022; 50¢) is a reprint of six articles written from Vietnam. See also her article "Suffer the Little Children," *Ladies Home Journal*, January 1967.

3. Robert Osgood, *Ideals and Self-Interest* (Chicago: 1953), p. 444.

4. Jonathan Randal, "Toll of Civilians Rising in Vietnam," *The New York Times*, April 21, 1967.

5. Richard Harwood, "Viet Civilian Toll Is Twice Army Rate," *Washington Post*, July 19, 1967.

6. Neil Sheehan, "Edward Kennedy Finds Vietnam Toll of Civilians High," *The New York Times*, May 8, 1967.

7. Harwood, *op. cit.*

8. Sheehan, *op. cit.*

9. *Ibid.*

10. Harwood, *op. cit.*

11. Public Opinion Survey, *The People of South Vietnam* (Princeton: 1965).

12. Senate Judiciary Committee, Refugee Subcommittee Report, *Refugee Problems in South Vietnam*, March 4, 1966. The Komer report (see

Chapter VIII, fn. 30) uses a slightly different figure: "700 of the 1,000 civilian doctors have been drafted."

13. Pepper, *op. cit.* Succeeding quotations and basic source are the same, except as otherwise cited, through page 124.

14. P. 41.

15. Senate Refugee Subcommittee, *op. cit.*

16. Martha Gellhorn, *op. cit.*, p. 4.

17. Hedrick Smith, "More Health Aid for Saigon Urged," *The New York Times*, September 22, 1967. The article summarizes the 100-page report of a Government-financed medical team headed by Dr. John H. Knowles, superintendent of the Massachusetts General Hospital, which made a three-week inspection trip to Vietnam.

18. "That a half million civilians may have been killed by Americans is a widely acknowledged statistic among our officials in Vietnam." Jonathan Mirsky, " 'The War Is Over,' " *Ramparts*, December 1967, p. 40.

19. "Heavy GI Casualties Suffered in 'Triangle,' " *Washington Post*, February 2, 1967.

20. Bernard B. Fall, " 'Unrepentant, Unyielding': An Interview with Viet Cong Prisoners," *New Republic*, February 4, 1967.

21. Press conference held at the Willard Hotel, Washington, February 2, 1967.

22. "I Have Seen the 'Destruction of a People I Love,' " *The New York Times*, September 24, 1967, p. E2.

23. Refugee Subcommittee, *op. cit.*, p. 12; see fn. 12 above.

24. Martha Gellhorn, *op. cit.*, p. 22 ff.; the article is titled "The Uprooted."

25. Charles Mohr, "U.S. Spray Planes Destroy Rice in Vietcong Territory," *The New York Times*, December 21, 1965. "The defoliation program has been going on since 1961."

26. See also Thomas O'Toole, "Chemical Warfare in Vietnam Called a Failure," *Washington Post*, November 13, 1967.

27. Charles Mohr, "Defoliation Unit Lives Perilously," *The New York Times*, December 20, 1965.

28. Eric Page, "Spray Killing of Enemy's Crops Stepped Up by U.S. in Vietnam," *The New York Times*, July 26, 1966. See also "Protests Fail to Deter Use of Viet Defoliants," *Washington Post*, October 21, 1966 (source of the 640,000-acre figure).

29. Carol Brightman, "The 'Weed Killers,' " *Viet Report*, June/July 1966, p. 39.

30. Sanche de Gramont, "Under Viet Cong Control," *Saturday Evening Post*, January 29, 1966.

31. William Beecher, "U.S. to Step Up Defoliation Missions in Vietnam," *The New York Times*, September 10, 1966. A Reuters dispatch from Saigon after the early 1967 "Tet" offensive indicates that the price of a human life has not risen in the intervening months: "A mother—$34. A young son or daughter—$17. Those, in the terrible economics of war, are

the prices of human lives, the value of government compensation for civilians killed in the battles that have ravaged the country for a month." *Washington Post*, "Viet Civilian Life Valued at $17 to $34," February 26, 1968.

32. William Beecher, "U.S. Might Step Up Use of Nonlethal Gas in Vietnam Fighting," *Wall Street Journal*, January 5, 1966.

33. Brightman, *op. cit.;* table, pp. 40–41.

34. University of Pennsylvania *Pennsylvanian;* quoted in Brightman, *op. cit.*, p. 43.

35. Max Frankel, "U.S. Reveals Use of Nonlethal Gas Against Vietcong," *The New York Times,* March 23, 1965.

36. Sydney *Morning-Herald*, January 13, 1966; cited in *I. F. Stone's Weekly*, January 31, 1966, which account says the Pentagon attributes the death to "lack of oxygen and smoke inhalation," rejecting the possibility that the "non-toxic" gas might have been causative.

37. J. A. Rothschild, *Tomorrow's Weapons* (New York: McGraw-Hill, 1964).

38. William S. Beller, "Forthright CBW Policy Urged," *Missiles and Rockets*, April 19, 1965.

39. Calculation: 1 mg. = .000035 oz., so 25 mg. = .0008 oz. With about 30 cubic meters of air in such a room, the total of Sarin needed would be .0024 oz. Another deadly agent, according to the *Washington Post* of March 25, 1968, probably "VX," was linked in March 1968 to "a mysterious wave of deaths" that finally killed some 7,000 sheep on lands 15 to 35 miles from Dugway Proving Ground, described as an Army test site and "the main center for field-testing chemical and biological war agents." The sheep began dying on March 14, one day after 320 gallons of a " 'persistent' nerve agent" were sprayed from a plane during a weekly "orientation" demonstration at Dugway. A full account may be found in three articles in the *Washington Post* by Victor Cohn: " 'Sea' of Dead Sheep Probed," March 21, 1968; "Nerve Gas at Sheep Site Reported by Sen. Moss," March 22; and "Did U.S. Army Nerve Gas Kill the 6,400 Sheep in Utah?," March 25.

40. Elinor Langer, "Chemical and Biological Warfare (II): The Weapons and the Policies," *Science*, January 20, 1967. This is the second of two parts which together provide the most comprehensive up-to-date source of CBW information available. The first part, "Chemical and Biological Warfare (I): The Research Program," appeared in the January 13 issue.

41. Rothschild, *op. cit.*, pp. 136–37.

42. Langer (I), January 13, 1967; fn. 40 above.

43. Thomas O'Toole, "Vietnam Plague Feared Spreading," *Washington Post*, February 24, 1968, p. A11.

44. R. R. Brubaker, E. D. Beesley, and M. J. Surgalla, "Pasteurella Pestis: Role of Pesticin I and Iron in Experimental Plague," *Science*, July 23, 1965.

45. Brightman, *op. cit.*, p. 14.

46. Langer (I), January 13, 1967.

47. Brightman, *ibid*.
48. Langer (I), January 13, 1967.

Chapter XI

1. Gallup poll, *The New York Times*, October 9, 1967.
2. Lyndon Johnson, *My Hope for America* (New York: 1964), pp. 65–66.
3. *The New York Times*, August 7, 1967.
4. *Washington Post*, June 4, 1967.
5. *The New York Times*, October 13, 1967.
6. Robert S. McNamara, "U.S. Is No 'Global Gendarme,'" *Washington Post*, December 3, 1967. Mr. McNamara's address to the American Society of Newspaper Editors was titled "Security in the Contemporary World." The *Post* reprint comprises "that part of his speech dealing with the developing nations," since this will be his concern as president of the World Bank.
7. *The New York Times*, May 19, 1967.
8. Public Opinion Survey, *The People of South Vietnam* (Princeton: 1965).
9. *The New York Times*, October 13, 1967.

In the fall of 1965, Senators Vance Hartke and J. William Fulbright had a chance meeting in Honolulu—a meeting that finally would precipitate the dramatic schism between the White House and the Senate Democratic majority. Unable to open a Senate Foreign Relations Committee hearing on the war in Vietnam, Senator Fulbright asked for Senator Hartke's help.

Syndicated columnists Rowland Evans and Robert Novak described what followed: "It was Indiana's Senator Hartke who wrote the letter to President Johnson, signed by sixteen Democratic Senators, protesting the resumption of the bombing of North Vietnam. It was Hartke who set strategy at secret sessions of the peace bloc." It was Senator Hartke, then, who provided the first main focus for Congressional dissent, and gave unity to the many forces opposing the Administration's conduct of the war.

The American Crisis in Vietnam is unlike any previous book. A step-by-step indictment by a man *inside* the government, this is a book that begins where others end. After tracing the background of the war from America's early massive economic support of the French in Indochina to our present-day total commitment, Senator Hartke reveals the whole range of damaging effects the war is having on America itself.

What happens to the democratic process when the public no longer knows when to believe what its government says? How has the war begun to destroy the fabric of our international relations throughout Europe and Asia? Senator Hartke shows how the war has damaged America and just how far-reaching the damage is.

Senator Hartke's views on these and other urgent questions rarely discussed openly by the government will startle many readers and add a new dimension to the way we think about the war in Vietnam.